The
Contemplative
Minister

Published by
The Bible Reading Fellowship
15 The Chambers, Vineyard
Abingdon, OX14 3FE
United kingdom
Tel: +44 (0)1865 319700
Email: enquiries@brf.org.uk
Website: www.brf.org.uk
BRF is a Registered Charity

ISBN 978 0 85746 360 9
First published 2015
10 9 8 7 6 5 4 3 2 1 0
All rights reserved

Acknowledgements
Unless otherwise stated, scripture quotations are taken from The New Revised
Standard Version of the Bible, Anglicised Edition, copyright © 1989, 1995 by the
Division of Christian Education of the National Council of the Churches of Christ
in the USA, are used by permission. All rights reserved.

Extracts from The Book of Common Prayer of 1662, the rights of which are
vested in the Crown in perpetuity within the United Kingdom, are reproduced by
permission of Cambridge University Press, Her Majesty's Printers.

Cover image: © Peter Kettle

Every effort has been made to trace and contact copyright owners for material
used in this resource. We apologise for any inadvertent omissions or errors, and
would ask those concerned to contact us so that full acknowledgement can be
made in the future.

A catalogue record for this book is available from the British Library

Printed and bound by CPI Group (UK) Ltd, Croydon CR0 4YY

The
Contemplative
Minister

Learning to lead from the still centre

Ian Cowley

Acknowledgements

This book could not have been written without the help and support of a number of friends and colleagues. 'The Contemplative Minister' started life as a day event which was offered as part of the Continuing Ministerial Development programme in the Diocese of Salisbury. I worked closely in setting this up with Sue Langdon and Darrell Weyman. Sue and Darrell have taught me an enormous amount about this way of living and ministering. This book would not have been possible without their friendship, wisdom and support.

Jane Charman, the Director of Ministry, has fully supported the development of this work, and has made it possible for us to run this programme. I want to thank all my colleagues in the Learning for Discipleship and Ministry Team, especially Tina Draycott, Andrea Dredge and Adrian Smale for their help.

A number of people have given invaluable advice along the way. I am particularly grateful to Anne Long, Andrew Judge, Aaron Kennedy and Paul Bradbury.

Sue Manners came to my aid at a critical point in the process of completing the manuscript. Her typing and attention to detail made a huge difference in getting this done on time.

I want to thank the team at BRF, especially Naomi Starkey and Kristina Petersen, who have enthusiastically supported this project from the start.

Alison, my wife, has shared the whole of my life as an ordained minister. She has lived with 'the book' for a long time, and without her love, care and support none of this would have been possible. Thank you, Alison, John and Grace. Praise be to God!

Contents

Foreword

THIS BOOK is concerned with the central vocation of those who are called to the ordained ministry. As priests, we are called to be people in whom others may see God. There is a great hunger for God among many people today. This is a hunger which is not just for things about God, for sermons, books, talks and videos, but for God himself. A contemplative minister is someone who is called first of all to God and to his heart of love, so that the world may also know God and his love for all that he has made.

God is the source of all life. In enabling people to see God, we enable them to know the One who is the giver of life, who is from eternity to eternity. Genesis 1:1 says, 'In the beginning, God…' We can't conceive of the beginning. 'But who made God?' ask our little darlings when we speak of these things to the children in our churches and schools. There never was a time when God was not. Our language is totally inadequate for this; it cannot contain the infinite mystery of God. Yet God calls those through whom he will make himself known to a hungry world. This is the wisdom of God, and it is our great privilege to be those through whom others may see and know the love of God.

In following our vocation to know God and to make him known, we have to live with paradox and mystery. God is infinite, and we are finite. 'My thoughts are not your thoughts,' says the Lord in Isaiah 55:8. In heaven we will want to tell everybody all the time our joy at our discovery of the divine nature. It will be just like being in love.

As priests we are exposed to the paradoxes of being familiar with God, and also the dangers of familiarity with holy things. In this great calling we are continually walking on holy ground. We ought to take off our shoes like Moses when God called him from the fire of the burning bush. We are both drawn to God and held back from him, like a moth before a lamp, like Peter before the great catch of fish. Peter cried out, 'Go away from me, Lord, for I am a sinful man!' (Luke 5:8). In God we encounter a mystery tremendous and fascinating. It both attracts us and pushes us back; it is too great for us. Yet God is continually offering us revelations of himself every day. Our response, like the wise men before the child Jesus, is to fall down and worship.

It is a grace and a mercy that God veils himself. When you have been in a dark dungeon, you can't rush out into bright sunlight and gaze on the sun. God is transcendent and he is also immanent. He has the whole world in his hands. God never leaves himself without witness. Now he has spoken fully and finally in the Son. 'Whoever has seen me has seen the Father,' says Jesus (John 14:9). He is the one who searches for the one lost sheep, which is probably not a lily-white lamb, but an obstreperous, dishevelled, rebellious sheep.

You don't need to impress God. You exist only because God has made you and loves you. God accepts us because he loves us. Think of a sick child whose mother sits up all night by their bed. So often we feel inadequate. Could God really love me like this? We don't feel accepted, and instead we feel anxious and insecure. Then we become dogmatic, bossy, hogging the limelight, hyper-sensitive to criticism. God gave Jesus all the praise and glory he needed. In knowing that God loves and accepts us, we find true freedom.

Friends, God loves you, from all eternity. You are not an accident; you are part of the divine plan. Every individual is unique, and God desires the love and contribution of every individual, like the triangle in the orchestra. Can you accept that you are accepted? There is true freedom in this, even if your neighbours disagree with you and oppose you.

God created us because he wanted to, not because he had to. Creation is the result of the overflowing of God's love. Creation is the object of the divine love which was, and is, and will be. This means that all of creation has an immeasurable value. Jesus says, 'The Father and I are one' (John 10:30), and yet I can wash the feet of my disciples.

For Jesus the cross was a leap of faith. Jesus walked the earth with the proper self-assurance of a human being, which comes from knowing that God loves us. This is as near to us as anything could be, but so often it doesn't sink into the very core of our being.

This brings an end to the obsessive dependence on the opinions of others. The cross is the mark of our discipleship. Suffering is the badge of all our tribe, as Shylock says in *The Merchant of Venice*. Jesus said that we would be hated as he was hated. We are going to share in the cross. 'Christ was trained in a carpenter's shop; and we persist in preferring a confectioner's shop,' said Evelyn Underhill (*The School of Charity*, Longmans, Green and Co, 1934, p. 40). A cross is an instrument of torture. If a church does not suffer, can it really claim to be the church of God?

If our churches are comfortable, we must worry. We are called to identification with those who are suffering; with the poor, the weak, the broken-hearted. The church has spoken too long from the perspective of the rich. This is what Jesus taught. Martyrdom means witnessing. God has given us in South Africa the privilege of witnessing, and it has been very costly. What do you do when so many of the laws of your country are unjust? What is the calling of the church when society keeps mixing up what is morally right and what is politically or economically expedient?

God calls us as his ministers to be witnesses, and he calls us to be faithful, not successful. We have a wonderful gospel if only we would believe it. God's love and mercy is so great. Let us not crush ourselves with harshness. We are not here to impress God. We are here to express praise and thanks for the love that God has showered upon us.

Let us relax. We leave all the problems and anxieties, the tensions, hurts and inadequacies, at the foot of the cross. We offer our joys and triumphs to be transmuted to God's praise and glory. God calls each of us to be a kind of Simon of Cyrene, carrying the cross of Jesus. This is the mystery of our calling, the privilege that is greater than anything we can put into words. God's love has been given to us, to be poured out in serving his beloved world.

God, you endow us with such infinite value.
I can only fall down and worship you.
Thou art God whose arms sustain the world.

Archbishop Desmond Tutu

Introduction

WHEN I WAS a parish priest in the Diocese of Natal in South
Africa, the Bishop of Natal invited Archbishop Desmond Tutu
to spend a day with the clergy of our diocese. Archbishop
Desmond spoke about events that were taking place in
South Africa at that troubled time. He spoke about the role
of the Church, and about the confidence we have in God,
who will ultimately triumph over all injustice, violence and
evil. Desmond also spoke to us about prayer, and about the
priority of prayer in our lives as ministers of the Church. He
said, 'Our people will not expect that we will be experts in
drains or in finance, but they will expect us to be experts in
prayer. And that is what they should expect from us.'

Archbishop Desmond Tutu is an outstanding example of a
contemplative minister. He is a man deeply rooted in prayer
and spiritual discipline, with a passionate concern for justice
and for all that hinders God's good and loving purposes for his
people. Being a contemplative minister is not likely to mean
living a quiet and stress-free life. This is not a call to sit in the
garden all day watching the flowers grow, although there may
well be times for that. Becoming a contemplative minister
is about being deeply rooted in God, and thus sharing his
concern and compassion for all that he has made.

'Deep calls to deep' says Psalm 42:7. Perhaps the most
important quality which is needed in Christian ministry
in contemporary Western culture is depth. Richard Foster
writes in his book *Celebration of Discipline*[1], 'In contemporary
society our Adversary majors in three things: noise, hurry
and crowds. If he can keep us engaged in "muchness" and

"manyness", he will rest satisfied.' We are a distracted and often weary generation, driving ourselves on from one complex set of demands to the next. There is no time for depth, because we are too busy with other things. Many of us know that this is not how we want to live, and we long for a way for our lives to be different. But how?

These questions have a particular urgency and relevance for all those involved in Christian ministry. For those who are seen by others to be God's ministers and the instruments of his peace, this is a tough call. Many Christian ministers occupy a dual identity; the public persona of the robed and respectable minister of religion, and the private world of struggle, frailty and weakness. For a considerable number the outcome is an unequal struggle to live up to seemingly impossible demands, leading sooner or later to burnout or bailout.

There was a time where Christian ministry offered, for those who were so inclined, the opportunity to spend one's life in the study of God's word, in reading and reflection, in prayer and sermon preparation, and in the quiet and faithful pastoral care of a community. The world has changed, and with it most of the expectations that govern Church appointments. These days there are very few jobs in full-time ministry which do not require a heroic combination of stamina, multitasking and change management.

I was recently asked to provide a reference for a friend who was applying for an appointment as rector of a group of small rural churches in a beautiful part of England. There were eleven questions on the form that I was asked to complete. The questions asked me to write about the candidate's gifts and weaknesses, and their ability to relate to people of different backgrounds and ages. Another question asked, 'How would you rate the candidate's ability to cope with pressure, a heavy workload and balancing the demands of work and personal life?' There were also questions about the ability to cope with conflict and whether the candidate had a sense of humour. There was nothing about prayer or prayerfulness.

I suspect that this reflects the reality of much contemporary full-time Christian ministry. How then are clergy and ministers to sustain and nurture their spiritual lives in the midst of a busy and demanding church or team of churches? The short answer is that it not easy. Ann Morisey says, 'I think the clergy task has become unsustainable.'[2] From my own experience of working with those in ordained ministry in the Anglican Diocese of Salisbury, I know that there are many who are looking for a better way of serving Christ than the relentless busyness and pressure which has become the norm for so many.

This book is about a different way of being in ministry. It is counter-cultural, because all authentic Christian discipleship is at its heart counter-cultural. Christians are called to be salt and light in our world: salt, which gives savour and prevents decay, and light, which drives out darkness and enables us to see things as they truly are. There is much in our world, and even in our church structures, that does not easily accept or understand a contemplative model for those in ministry. But for many, this is not just a matter of differing models of professional ministerial formation, but a matter of sheer survival. The Church needs to recognise anew in every age what it is asking of those it sets aside and ordains for the task of pastoral ministry and leadership. For the Anglican Church this is set out in the services of ordination. The Book of Common Prayer provides a particularly rich and enduring template for the meaning of ordained ministry as understood by the Church through many generations.

In the service of the ordering (or ordination) of priests or presbyters in the Book of Common Prayer, the bishop reads his charge to the candidates immediately before they are asked to make their ordination promises. He exhorts them to have in remembrance 'into how high a dignity, and to how weighty an office and charge ye are called: that is to say, to be messengers, watchmen, and stewards of the Lord.' Then, having described the wholly consecrated life and work to which the ordained person is called, the bishop says, 'We have good hope that... you have clearly determined, by God's grace, to give yourselves wholly to this office, whereunto it hath pleased God to call you: so that, as much as lieth in you, you will apply yourselves wholly to this one thing, and draw all your cares and studies this way; and that you will continually pray to God the Father...'

These are strong words, of great seriousness and consequence. Every time I come back to them, I find them deeply moving and impressive. These words continue to speak of what ordination means, for me personally, and for those with whom I work who are exploring the possibility of ordained ministry for themselves.

What does this mean in the context of Western culture in the 21st century? How do we make the connections between the enduring and still compelling call to pastoral and priestly ministry, and the demands of a world of relentless activity and the unlimited availability of information? Can we who are ordained ministers of the Gospel still see ourselves as having a calling to be 'holy men and women' who are able to point others to the grace and presence of the living God because we ourselves are living in first-hand knowledge of this truth and reality? These questions are the reason that this book has been written.

Part One

Vocation

Chapter 1

Being and doing

'I will not give you counsel, saying do this or do that. For not in doing or contriving, nor in choosing between this course and another can I avail; but only in knowing what was and what is and in part also what shall be.'

J.R.R. TOLKIEN, *THE LORD OF THE RINGS*[3]

IN THE MID-1970s, when I was a student in South Africa, I first began to explore a call to full-time ordained ministry in the Anglican Church. This was not something that I had ever envisaged as a possible career choice. It was not a possibility that had seemed even remotely attractive to me as a young person leaving school. During my student days at the University of Natal I was drawn into the life and work of a number of university Christian organisations, and I began to encounter something which was profoundly attractive and life-changing. I saw a new community, an alternative society that at its centre was radically different from the established order of apartheid South Africa. I increasingly knew that this was what I wanted to do with my life: to be part of a Church which would be the hope of the nation, the salt and light in a land that desperately needed justice and transformation.

I made an appointment to see the local bishop, Kenneth Hallowes, at his office in Pietermaritzburg, Natal. Bishop Ken already knew me well, and he knew that God was calling me. He made the decision to accept me as an ordination candidate of the diocese, and agreed that I should travel to England to train at one of the theological colleges there. Shortly before I left for England I went to see Bishop Ken again. I suspect he knew that I was a serious minded-young man, determined to make a difference by offering my life in the service of Christ. So he said to me before I left his office that day, 'Remember, Ian, being comes before doing.'

Those words have stayed with me and have been increasingly important to me over the years: 'Being comes before doing.' I have wrestled often, in different times and situations, with the balance between being and doing. My natural instinct is to be doing, to be making things happen, getting things done. I quickly discovered, though, that unless I made time for being, I began to run into difficulty. I would find a weariness and a frustration rising up in me to the point that it threatened to overwhelm me. I found myself like a swimmer in the open sea, only just keeping my head above the waves and the deep water. Surely this was not how it was meant to be.

In the years leading up to the birth of a democratic South Africa in 1994, we went through some exceptionally testing and traumatic times. During those days many of us who were part of the Church in South Africa found ourselves on the frontline of working for justice and reconciliation, in prophetic witness and in care for the poor and the suffering. No one can live through times such as those without experiencing a lot of stress and pain. Following Christ was never going to be easy or comfortable. How do we survive in ministry when the going gets really tough? I knew that my greatest need was to be more and more deeply rooted in the unfailing and unconditional love of God which is offered to us in Christ.

Gradually my understanding of God's call to me as a priest and minister in the Anglican Church has changed. During the 1980s, when I was rector of a church in a suburban setting on the edge of Pietermaritzburg, I came to realise very clearly that I could not do the work of ministry unless I was, first and foremost, a person of prayer. Prayer had to become the priority of my life. To know God, and to live in relationship with God, was my first call. This had to come first, even before growing the Church or serving the poor or standing for justice. I would only be able to sustain the work to which I knew I had been called if I lived each day in active dependence and trust in God.

Indeed, I could see from those around me that the cost of taking on the work of being an activist in the service of the Lord and of justice and the poor could be very high. In such demanding contexts, unless we are deeply sustained by the resources which only Christ can give us, we are all too likely to lose our way, and perhaps even lose our vocation. Joan Chittister wrote, 'We have to remember that work is not prayer. It is at best an extension of prayer. We fool ourselves if we argue that we don't have to pray because we work so hard or our work is so good. Those who work without prayer—no matter how good the work, no matter how sincere the minister—soon dry up inside. They have nothing left to give. Or, the work fails and they have no faith to sustain them, no perspective to encourage them.'[4]

In the Diocese of Salisbury I help to lead regular days for those in ministry entitled 'The Contemplative Minister'. The starting point for all that I teach on these days is this: the heart of priestly ministry is the call to an ever deepening relationship of love for God, to lead others into that relationship and to enable them to respond to God in loving service and mission. The heart of our call, very simply, is to know God and to teach our people to pray and to respond to

God's call. Being comes before doing. Ministry is primarily about who you are, not about what you do.

The question that many of us are struggling with is this: how do we live this out? The demands of our role and the expectations placed upon us by others and by ourselves drive us on until we cry out to find a better way of being in ministry. Many times, in the midst of these pressures and demands, I have tried somehow to hold to the promise of Jesus in Matthew 11:28: 'Come to me all you that are weary and are carrying heavy burdens, and I will give you rest.'

In working this out, it has been important for me to be reminded that Jesus says in Luke 9:25, 'What does it profit someone if they gain the whole world and lose or forfeit their true self?' My experience of seeking to live a life of following Jesus is that Jesus is calling me to discover and to become my true self. It is only in becoming my true self that I will find the rest that Jesus promises. Yet the responsibilities of public ministry can make this very difficult. Thomas Merton, the great contemplative writer and thinker, wrote about the tension between the true self and the false self. Merton also wrote a chapter entitled 'Being and Doing',[5] and he points to the connection between finding my true self and finding the right balance for each of us in our being and our doing.

What is the false self? Merton identifies the false self as the person we wish to present to the world, and the person we want the world to revolve around.[6] Richard Rohr, in his book *Adam's Return*, says, 'Our false self is who we *think* we are. It is our mental self-image and social agreement, which most people spend their whole lives living up to—or down to. It is all a fictional creation. It will die when we die. It is endlessly fragile, needy, and insecure, and it is what we are largely dealing with in the secular West.'[7]

The false self is the part of us that is most concerned with outward appearances, with appearing strong, or self-confident or successful or busy.

If my main concern in any situation is 'What are people thinking of me? How do I appear to them?' then it is likely that my false self is playing a major role. In parish ministry we can easily find ourselves constantly responding to the pressures of meeting other peoples' expectations. Inevitably some people want to see their minister keeping busy, working hard, growing the church, visiting the church members, producing results. These are some of the expectations that constantly attend the lives of those in public ministry.

We also have to deal with the pressure of our own expectations of ourselves. Many of us are in full-time ministry at least partly because of our own personal history. This may well include a need to be needed or to be seen to 'be good'. It is important that we become familiar with the inner expectations which drive us and make us who we are. These may well be inherited from important figures in our childhood and youth, our parents, our teachers, even our friends and siblings.

Finding our true selves means moving away from those parts of ourselves that are mainly concerned with proving ourselves to others, whether they be our parishioners and colleagues or figures from our past who may even no longer be alive. Christ calls us to freedom. 'You will know the truth, and the truth will make you free,' says Jesus (John 8:32). In becoming my true self I am set free in Christ to be the person I truly am, the real Ian. I am set free from all that hinders me in being close to God who loves me unconditionally and accepts me as the person that he made me to be.

In his book *New Seeds of Contemplation*, Thomas Merton

describes how so much of our energy can be used up in trying to maintain the agenda and the demands of the false self. Merton writes, 'Thus I use up my life in the desire for pleasures and the thirst for experiences, for power, honour, knowledge and love, to clothe this false self and construct its nothingness into something objectively real. And I wind experiences around myself and cover myself with pleasures and glory like bandages in order to make myself perceptible to myself and to the world, as if I were an invisible body that could only become visible when something visible covered its surface.'[8] Merton's life as a Trappist monk and hermit points us to our own need to look beyond the incessant demands and expectations of others and of our society, and to seek the depths that lie within. However, Merton is also clear that we find our true selves only through love and selflessness, and in relationship and in communion with others.

A better way

The false self is preoccupied with outward appearance, with what other people think about us and about what we are doing. Success and achievement become important because they seem to define our identity and give us a sense of significance. Gradually many of us discover how much of this is hollow, and increasingly we see it for the illusion that it is. No matter how hard we try to fill our lives with more experiences, more achievements, more power and influence, somehow we are no closer to finding real and lasting value or significance. Prestige and influence in society are fleeting, and their pursuit pits us against one another and makes us compare and compete, to very little real and lasting effect.

Surely there is a better way, especially for those set aside by the Church to live the example of Christ. A few years ago the Bishop of Salisbury invited Timothy Radcliffe, the Dominican priest, writer and teacher, to spend Lent in the diocese, and to meet with small groups of clergy to reflect on important issues in our vocation and ministry. Timothy Radcliffe asked us, 'How did we get from sabbath to the Protestant work ethic?' He spoke to us about the violence of busyness and rush, and said that it is important for us to be seen to rest with God. 'We are those who believe that salvation is through grace, not works,' he said. He reminded us of the importance of 'divine leisure': hanging around with God. Timothy said that we need to remember who we are in Christ and refuse to be workaholics.

David Stancliffe, at that time the Bishop of Salisbury, reminded us of the words of St Irenaeus (c.112–c.202), 'The glory of God is a human being fully alive.' David Stancliffe then said to the gathering of clergy, 'Our words will only have authority if we are alive. The question is, "How may you have a life?"'

Becoming a contemplative minister is about taking this question seriously. At the heart of this vision of ministry is the call to become human beings who have discovered what it is to be fully alive in Christ. Our priority will become finding that which is life-giving for us and for those whom we serve. It is also about turning away from all that is life-draining and life-destroying for us and for those around us. We will have to face the insidious demands of the false self, and be willing to choose life and freedom instead of choosing the pursuit of success, pleasure and significance. We will need to be willing to get to grips with the deeper realities of personal transformation, so that we may find our true selves in Christ. Then, by our being in Christ, our doing will speak to those around us of life and peace.

Chapter 2

Knowing our vocation

As Jesus passed along the Sea of Galilee, he saw Simon and his brother Andrew casting a net into the sea—for they were fishermen. And Jesus said to them, 'Follow me and I will make you fish for people.' And immediately they left their nets and followed him. As he went a little farther, he saw James son of Zebedee and his brother John, who were in their boat mending the nets. Immediately he called them; and they left their father Zebedee in the boat with the hired men, and followed him.

MARK 1:16–20

The reason to wake up

THE WORD 'vocation' literally means 'calling'. Finding one's vocation is not only something that is important for Christians and for the work of ministry; vocation is for everyone. We all have a vocation, a calling in life. The Scottish comedian, Billy Connolly, says, 'I try to tell my children, "Just try to see what you're drawn to—the type of store window you're drawn to" because it's no mistake when you're drawn. Something's telling you, "This is the direction you should be going." It might be pet shops, it might be funeral parlours. Just try to notice what you're drawn to all the time. Because that's the way your life should go. And when you do something that you feel vocationally drawn to, it's not like a job. It's the reason to wake, and you wake up feeling good in the morning, which is a wonderful thing.'[9]

It is very important to find our vocation, our calling, in life. When you have found your vocation, you can wake up in the morning knowing that your life has meaning and a purpose. You know, deep within yourself, that in one way or another you will be using your God-given gifts to do something that is worthwhile and life-giving for yourself and for other people. Finding our vocation is about finding what it is that gives us life. This is God's purpose for each and every one of us. Jesus said, 'I came that they may have life, and have it abundantly' (John 10:10).

Finding one's vocation does not mean that life will never be challenging or testing. Jesus certainly did not promise that following him would be the way to an easy life. If we are living vocationally, we will develop an inner resilience and sense of purpose that will sustain us through all the difficulties and obstacles that we may face.

So an important question for each of us is this: 'What is it that is life-giving for you?' If we can find that which brings life to us and to those around us, then we will surely have found that to which we are being called.

A second question is this, 'What is it that you love to do?' John Adair has written a book called *How to find your vocation: A guide to discovering the work you love*. He writes, 'At its simplest, vocational people have found the work they love to do. They may use the word love in conversation about their work or some aspect of it. They are extremely reluctant to give it up.'[10]

Recently I was listening to an interview on the radio with the singer Tom Jones. I first heard of Tom Jones in the 1960s, when he had a hit with his song 'It's not unusual'. Today, nearly 50 years later, he is still recording and singing, and in this interview he was asked how he had been able to sustain his career over so many years. This is what he said: 'I really love to sing. It's like breathing to me.'

When Simon and Andrew and James and John were called by Jesus, and they left everything and followed him, it seems clear that they knew within themselves that they were being called not just by a way of life or an occupation, but by a person. They recognised that Jesus is himself the way and the truth and that he is life. We find life above all in knowing Christ and in following him. His first disciples recognised that in him the deepest longings of their hearts would be met, and that he would give a new dimension of meaning and purpose to their lives. It is important always to remember that for Christians ultimately our call is not to a job or a ministry or even to a way of life. It is to a person, to Jesus Christ the Lord.

For all those in Christian ministry, this is the key to keeping our vocation alive. Our relationship with Christ, our desire to know Christ and to increase daily in love for Christ will sustain us in serving him. This is where vocation and spirituality are directly and inextricably linked. It is the being and doing of ministry.

It is because God loves us that we are called in the first place, although we may not articulate our call in this way. It was because Jesus called his disciples in unconditional acceptance and love for them that they were able to respond by leaving everything and following him. We too are called first of all from God's heart of love and compassion for each one of us. He wants the very best for us; his desire is that we fulfil all our God-given potential by becoming our true selves in his service.

The spirituality of vocation

The value of what we *do* will flow directly from who we *are*. In the work of the kingdom of God, spirituality and vocation are two sides of the same coin. You cannot have one without the other. Yet the danger is that we become preoccupied by the tasks we face, and by the appearance of giftedness or competence. We are told in 1 Samuel 16:7 that we 'look on the outward appearance but the Lord looks on the heart'. What matters to Jesus is what is in our hearts. In the life of Jesus we see again and again that he is primarily concerned with our attitudes, motives, desires and values. Jesus is scathing in his comments about those whose main concern is outward religious observance. At the centre of the vocation to ministry is spiritual formation, paying attention to our interior life—the care of the soul—and helping others as fellow pilgrims.

For Christians, spiritual formation means being formed into the likeness of Jesus for the sake of others. To know Christ is to become more like him, day by day. This is not something we can do by our own strength and willpower but is all about grace. It begins when we recognise how in need of God's grace we are, and how much we need Christ to be formed in us. God meets us where we are, not where we would like to be or where we would like other people to think we are.

In truth, Christ is already in us. Paul speaks of 'the riches of the glory of this mystery, which is Christ in you, the hope of glory' (Colossians 1:27). Our need is to become who we are in Jesus. As we follow him, the old hard shell of the false self cracks open, and deep within us the shoots of new life spring up and transform our hearts and our lives.

The spirituality of vocation is concerned with the being rather than the doing of the person who is called. Unless we are clear that we are called first of all to pay attention to our being in Christ, we will struggle to keep our vocation alive. How can we survive, let alone flourish, if, week after week, we are giving our best energies to doing the work of ministry, to activity and busyness? As ministers of Christ, we have to be clear in our own minds that we have been called first of all to a relationship with our Lord. Unless that relationship is being nurtured and sustained, we will be failing in our vocation.

This is challenging for many of us because it is so contrary to our prevailing culture. Our society is preoccupied with success and achievement. There seems to me to be an increasing pressure even in the church to measure the results and outcomes of all that we are doing. 'How can something be successful if we cannot measure the results?' we are asked. Prayer and being and the ways of the kingdom of God do not lend themselves easily to such measurement.

Integrity

Christian vocation and ministry must be rooted in integrity. The opposite of integrity is hypocrisy or deceit, pretending to be something that we are not. The minister who stands before a congregation on Sunday morning and tries to preach a sermon which is not true to their own inner life is not likely to see much fruit. People usually know when we are trying to be something that is not true to who we really are.

Integrity means living out the truth of who I am before God. It is the key to any relationship with God. To be able to enter the presence of God, we simply have to stop pretending.

Jesus said, 'Whenever you pray, go into your room and shut the door and pray to your Father who is in secret; and your Father who is in secret will reward you' (Matthew 6:6). An old saying that I came across many years ago remains true: 'What you are on your knees before God, that is what you are and nothing more.' Psalm 51:6 says of God, 'You desire truth in the inward being; therefore teach me wisdom in my secret heart.'

Again and again Jesus speaks of the importance to God of what is in our hearts. He takes the commandments concerning adultery and murder and says that it is the lust and anger that is in our hearts that is sinful before God (Matthew 5:22, 27–28). In Matthew 15 Jesus speaks of the things that defile a person before God. It is not a matter of ceremonial, of foods that are clean or unclean; but 'out of the heart come evil intentions, murder, adultery, fornication, theft, false witness, slander. These are what defile a person, but to eat with unwashed hands does not defile' (Matthew 15:19–20).

Living as a contemplative minister means that we accept certain core spiritual disciplines in order that God by his Holy Spirit may break the hold of the illusions we have about ourselves. We are on a journey towards truthfulness in the inward being, led by the Spirit who is himself 'the Spirit of truth' (John 14:17). This is why spiritual disciplines are so important. Discipline is what we need for grace to be worked out in our hearts and our lives.

To keep our vocation alive requires close attention to our inner life, the life that is hidden with Christ in God. This requires the daily observance of foundational spiritual disciplines, as a primary commitment in the life of the minister. This may well have been understood better in past generations than it is today. Certainly there have been times when the Church's understanding of the priest or pastor was first of all that they would be a holy person, someone called and set aside to spend much time in prayer, in worship, and reading and the study of the scriptures. A holy person is someone who has a depth of relationship with God that is clearly discernible, even if it is hard to quantify. This of course is also the primary quality required in anyone who exercises a ministry of spiritual direction, accompanying others on their spiritual journey.

As I look at the job descriptions of many paid ministry roles, it seems that this quality of holiness is no longer the central focus in ministry. The task seems to have become the priority. The life of prayer is in danger of being seen as secondary, as almost a luxury for which, generally, there will not be much time available because of all the apparently more important things that need to be done. The problem is that if we give up on prayer, it becomes very difficult to keep alive any true sense of vocation to Christian ministry.

Listening to many of the ministers that I work with in Salisbury Diocese, it is clear to me that the idea of becoming a contemplative minister is becoming ever more timely and important. Our culture is in desperate need of role models who are able to practise a life of prayer, who have time for stillness, and who are deeply secure in their knowledge of God's unconditional love. This is not to say that we will not be busy or that we will not face many demands. However, the very core of the vocation of the Christian minister is to be a holy person, a woman or man set aside for closeness to God. We will look at this in more detail in the next chapter.

In a world that is hungry for a spirituality which makes a difference to daily life, for mindfulness and for meditation, we are those who should be the teachers of prayer in each of our communities, to whom people should instinctively turn when they want to know more about the life of prayer. As followers of Christ, we are those who can show by our lives that true prayer is not simply a matter of personal well-being but is the inner strength and motivation that leads us directly to service and the world's needs. That is true contemplative ministry.

Part Two

Contemplative ministry

Chapter 3

Becoming a contemplative minister

O God, who hast prepared for them that love thee such good things as pass man's understanding: Pour into our hearts such love toward thee, that we, loving thee above all things, may obtain thy promises, which exceed all that we can desire; through Jesus Christ our Lord. Amen

THE COLLECT: THE SIXTH SUNDAY AFTER TRINITY, THE BOOK OF COMMON PRAYER

IN 2008, after 30 years in parish ministry in South Africa and in England, I moved to a new role in the Church. I was appointed Coordinator of Vocations and Spirituality for the Anglican Diocese of Salisbury. The work of this diocese covers most of the counties of Wiltshire and Dorset in southern England, a beautiful but large and diverse geographical area. A lot of my work has been in helping men and women to explore their sense of vocation, of how God may be calling them to live and to respond to his call in service and ministry.

I have also done a lot of work in helping to resource those in ministry, whether lay or ordained, to sustain their vocation and to keep their spiritual lives growing. Our starting point is always that vocation is for everyone. As mentioned in Chapter 2, we all have a vocation, and there should be no hierarchy or status issue involved. Our vocation and ministry may be lay or ordained, in leadership or in supporting others who lead. It may be in administration, in pastoral work, in music, in working with children and young people, and in countless other ways of serving.

Vocation always means serving. When we find our vocation, we will find ourselves serving and blessing other people in some way or other. Barack Obama, in his first inauguration address, spoke about the American heroes who 'embody the spirit of service; the willingness to find meaning in something greater than themselves'. It is a wonderful thing to discover your vocation and the joy of serving others and making a difference in our world. Every one of us can be an agent of transformation, in our own families, our own communities, our nation and our world.

For some with whom I work in exploring their vocation, there is a clear sense of call to ordained ministry. This could be as an ordained deacon or as a priest or presbyter. The discernment and confirmation of this call by the Church usually takes quite a long time. It is a serious and careful process, which involves a number of wise and well-trained people, who together will help to confirm that we believe that this person is truly called by God to this ministry. When that call is recognised and confirmed by the Church, there is great rejoicing. It's wonderful to share with a group of women and men at the great service of ordination when, after years of discernment, preparation and training, they are set apart by the whole Church to the life and work of the ordained ministry.

After a few years in the work of the ordained ministry, questions and difficulties often come to the surface. For many, the joy and excitement of training and ordination gradually fade into the past, as new questions and doubts arise. Some find themselves asking, 'How do I keep my vocation alive? This is far more difficult and demanding than I ever expected. Why didn't they tell me at theological college that it would be like this?' A few years ago I met up with a young man whom I had known during his days at theological college. I asked him how he was finding parish ministry. He said, 'No one ever told me how utterly tedious parish ministry would be.'

Some of this will be due to the particular circumstances with which ministers have to deal. They may be faced with a number of small rural congregations where the main concerns seem to be the annual fundraising effort or the repairs to the church roof. Maybe there will be difficult colleagues or local leaders. One priest I know, a man with a large beard, arrived at a new church. The churchwarden, who had been there many years, came to visit him. 'Welcome to St Mary's,' he said. We're pleased that the bishop has found us a priest at last. Just one thing—you have until Sunday to remove that beard.'

In situations like this many will start to wonder whether their call is no longer to local church ministry and leadership. Maybe they got it wrong, and this is not what they were called to after all. 'This is just not me; I can't do this,' some will be thinking. A recent survey quoted in *The Times* said that 'nearly half of 500 clergy polled recently said that they needed or wanted help with managing stress, while twelve per cent described themselves as struggling or barely coping. Two thirds of those said that they "very frequently" thought of giving up.'[11] Other surveys have shown that job satisfaction for a lot of clergy remains high, and for many there is still a sense of the deep privilege of this way of life. My perception is that every year it is becoming more difficult to find parishes where clergy can thrive and exercise a primarily pastoral and contemplative ministry.

In a lot of parishes one is faced with the constant need to be an agent of transformation in communities that are often deeply resistant to change. A while ago I was speaking to an archdeacon from a diocese in central England, and I asked him if he knew of any interesting parish appointments or vacancies that were available. He said that the only jobs that he had to offer were what he called 'remedial'—in other words, sorting out problems and introducing change.

There can be no doubt that it is tough out there for parish clergy in the Church of England. That has certainly been my own experience. The demands are numerous, and often there is little support or affirmation. This is not just a problem for the Church of England. Across all denominations the levels of stress and drop-out among those in pastoral ministry are far too high.

How then are those in full-time ministry to survive? Our hope, surely, should be that we are not aiming simply to survive, but that we expect to flourish and to find our work deeply fulfilling. The Diocese of Salisbury has for some years now invested heavily in programmes to nurture and sustain the well-being of the clergy. This has been hugely important and helpful for many of us in ministry and leadership. In my own role in the diocese I have been responsible for programmes that develop the spirituality of well-being. All of this is concerned with the question: what will enable us to thrive in ministry?

As we have spoken to hundreds of clergy and ministers about this, it has become clear that many of us have a longing to live as contemplative ministers. We long to find ways of living that will enable us to be so deeply rooted in God's love that we will be able to sustain the demanding role which the Church now asks us to fulfil. This has involved getting to grips with the issues of personal transformation and the false self, as I have already noted. It has also meant looking carefully at our models of ministry and priesthood, and making some important choices about how we will live out our vocation in the parishes and jobs in which we find ourselves.

First things first

The key to living out our vocation is to put first things first. What are the 'first things' for those called to a life of pastoral ministry? This is the starting point for all that I teach on our Contemplative Ministry days: the heart of priestly ministry is, first, the call to an ever deepening relationship of love for God, and, second, to lead others into that relationship and to enable them to respond to God in loving service and mission. The heart of our vocation is to know God and to teach our people to pray and to respond to God's call.

Our first call is to God. 'The chief end of man is to glorify God and to enjoy him forever,' says the Westminster Shorter Catechism. We are called to be those who specialise in knowing God and walking with God through all that life brings. We are called also to be those who are living our own lives in such a way that others will know that God's love in Christ is the enduring truth in all our human experience. If it's not true and real for us, it's not likely that we will be able to communicate anything more than a few platitudes.

Our call is not only to know God but to enjoy him forever. We are to find time to enjoy God, to gaze at the beauty of all that he has made, to bless him and thank him and worship him from our hearts. When the spirit of worship and thanksgiving dries up, something vital to the whole work of ministry is lost. Jesus said, '"You shall love the Lord your God with all your heart, and with all your soul, and with all your mind." This is the greatest and first commandment. And a second is like it: "You shall love your neighbour as yourself." On these two commandments hang all the law and the prophets' (Matthew 22:37–39). Both of these commandments are essential; you cannot have one without the other. But we must put first things first, and the first commandment is that we are to love God with all our heart and mind and soul and strength.

Loving God

What does it mean to love God? The word 'love' is not straightforward when it is applied to our relationship with God. It is easy to say that we love God, but how do we show that we truly love someone? If I love another person, I will want to spend a great deal of time with him or her. I will want to please them, to offer them gifts, to help them in whatever needs doing that is important to them. Above all, I will want to be close to them, to be where they are, and to share in their experience of life and the world.

The uncomfortable truth for many of us is that, although we do love God and long to know him more and to serve him more, most of the time we are far more concerned about ourselves and our own interests and feelings and comfort. Our first instinct, again and again, is to self-interest, self-promotion and self-preservation. This takes us back to the false self which is always with us. The ways of the false self have to be unlearnt, slowly and often painfully. Thomas Merton says, 'For me to be a saint means to be myself.'[12] Learning to love God with all our hearts is a lifetime's journey, and it is also the journey towards becoming my true self. The two journeys are in fact one.

When we are ordained, we are set aside to a life of knowing God and of living and speaking for him to his people and to the world. This doesn't just happen by a kind of holy magic or through some miraculous grace given in the ordination service. It is true that grace is given through our ordination, and especially that we are given the gift of the Holy Spirit without whom we can do none of this, but we also have to do our part. We have to go to wherever God calls us, and to live lives of such holy discipline and love that God's grace will be able to flow through our human weakness to his people and to his world. Unless we live disciplined and consecrated lives, we will not be able to be the instruments of his peace.

We have to make choices. What does it mean to say that prayer is the priority of my life? Am I committed to a daily discipline of prayer and the reading and study of the Bible? This is what was placed before me at my ordination, and it is at the heart of the Book of Common Prayer ordination service. When I was ordained in the Anglican Church in South Africa, it was made clear to me that it was a matter of obligation for all priests to say morning and evening prayer each day, unless prevented by sickness or some other unavoidable reason. Nonetheless it took me some years to accept fully that a daily time alone with God was an essential discipline that I had to maintain, if possible every single day of my life. It had to be like having breakfast or cleaning my teeth. I simply cannot sustain the life of ministry without this.

Putting first things first in ministry means that we make the nurture of our relationship with God the priority of our lives. Daily prayer becomes a non-negotiable personal discipline. It is all too easy to pay lip service to this principle, but the challenge is for us to practise what we affirm as being of first importance. This is likely to be a process of development over time, as we learn from others and find what it is that draws us into life.

For many years I have aimed to plan one day a month as a personal Quiet Day, when I go to a place where I can be alone and spend the day praying, listening, reading and reflecting upon my life and ministry. Silence and solitude are vital in the deepening of our experience of God, and we must make time and space for this. I also take an annual silent retreat, usually in a Christian retreat centre or religious community. This is an important way of spending a more sustained time away from the noise and demands of everyday life, when I can draw close to God and be renewed in my love for him.

Be true to your vocation

If we are called to give our lives to the work of pastoral ministry, then it is important that we are clear about what this means. At the heart of pastoral ministry are three tasks:

- Prayer
- Pastoral care
- Preaching and teaching the word of God

Being a contemplative minister means being faithful to these three central commitments over the whole of our life's ministry. Not everyone is called to this work. Some are called to be evangelists, some administrators, some prophets who work in the service of justice and the poor. The presbyter, the pastor and the priest are called and ordained to these three tasks, and everything else flows from this. Perhaps it is why all ordained ministers in the Anglican Church have to spend three of four years working in a local church as curates before going on to any other wider or more specialised ministry, such as being hospital or military chaplains or teaching at a university.

The service of ordination in the Book of Common Prayer sets out these three priorities for those who are to be ordained as priests or presbyters. They are asked, 'Will you be diligent in prayers, and in reading of the holy scriptures, and in such studies as help to the knowledge of the same, laying aside the study of the world and the flesh?' The answer is, 'I will endeavour myself so to do, the Lord being my helper.'

They are charged to be 'messengers, watchmen, and stewards of the Lord; to teach and to premonish, to feed and provide for the Lord's family; to seek for Christ's sheep that are dispersed abroad'. Then they are solemnly told, 'Have always therefore printed in your remembrance, how great a treasure is committed to your charge. For they are the sheep of Christ, which he bought with his death, and for whom he shed his blood.'

Herein lies the true vocation, the true calling, of all those who are ordained priest. There is much besides this, of course, but if we neglect these core tasks, we fail both God and our own vocation.

My experience in 30 years of parish ministry is that through faithfulness to these three tasks—prayer, preaching and pastoral care—the rest of the work has somehow fallen into place. There are many other things which will need to be done when we have the responsibility of leading a church or churches. Faithfulness to prayer, to pastoral work, and to the diligent preaching of God's word will mean that we have fulfilled the trust given to us by God and by his Church.

In my experience, healthy churches are usually, if not always, those where the pastor or priest is clearly a person of prayer, who cares for and visits the flock, and teaches the scriptures faithfully, week in and week out. There may well be growth; sometimes for various reasons the numbers decline, but that is in God's hands. Our responsibility is to be faithful to the calling we have been given, to the best of our ability. Everything else we can then leave to God.

Engagement and disengagement

Some years ago I was encouraged to keep a careful note of how I used my time during one full week in parish ministry. I wrote down how I spent each hour, and then at the end of the week I reflected on the amount of time I had spent on the various tasks and commitments of the work, and the other things that I had done with my time. I recommend doing something like this on an annual basis. We learn a lot about ourselves when we look carefully at the realities of how we actually allocate our time.

What I found was that I used a surprisingly large amount of time in various forms of administration and tasks which had to be done so that the organisation of the church would continue and run smoothly. Meetings also took a lot of my time. I spent comparatively little time in one-to-one meetings with members of the church, and comparatively little time in prayer, reading and study of the scriptures. An important goal for me became to try to decrease the proportion of my time I spent in tasks and meetings, and to spend more of my time and energy on the crucial work of prayer, study of the Bible and pastoral ministry.

I have found it helpful to aim at a proper balance of engagement and disengagement in ministry. This was clearly important for Jesus. We are told that 'many crowds would gather to hear him and to be cured of their diseases. But he would withdraw to deserted places and pray' (Luke 5:15–16). It seems that Jesus regularly made time to go up into the mountains or to a quiet place to pray and listen to his Father's voice (see Matthew 14:23; Luke 4:42; 9:28; Mark 6:46; 9:2). This was not something which Jesus occasionally found time to do. It was his regular, probably daily, discipline and practice. If this was important for Jesus, how much more will it be for those of us who are his followers and ministers.

Finding the balance between engagement and disengagement will be different for each of us. Some of us are extroverts who gain our energy from being with people, while others are introverts who need time and space on their own to renew their energy and enthusiasm for being engaged with people and their needs. There must be some disengagement for each of us if we are to have time for prayer, for knowing God and listening to him. In our contemporary culture the overwhelming pressure is to be doing too much, to be overly engaged in doing and not sufficiently invested in being.

What is the right balance for those in ministry? Bill Hybels in his book *Courageous Leadership* has some interesting things to say about this. Bill is the founder and leader of Willow Creek Community Church in Illinois and one of the most respected church leaders in America. He describes how he was reading an article by acclaimed leadership expert Dee Hock and was shocked to discover that Hock recommends that leaders should give 50 per cent of their time to the tasks of self-management. Hock says, 'It is management of self that should occupy 50 per cent of our time and the best of our ability.' As Bill Hybels pondered and reflected on what Hock was saying, he realised his need to change his own priorities radically. Hybels quotes the words spoken to him by three advisors who came to see him on behalf of the church. They said to him, 'The best gift you can give the people you lead here at Willow is a healthy, energised, fully surrendered and focussed self. And no one can make that happen in your life except you. It's up to you to make the right choices so that you can be at your best.'[13]

Interestingly, this is the model that was given to me for my own use of time when I left the theological college in Oxford where I trained for the ministry. In our final term at college, before we were all sent out to be ordained and to start work in our new churches and parishes, the principal led us in a series of leavers' classes. In these classes he gave us a lot of practical advice and wisdom about how we should deal with the various demands and issues that we would face in parish ministry. He spoke about the use of our time, and gave us a suggestion of a basic plan for priestly ministry. Sundays are busy and important days because that is when we see our people and have the opportunity to conduct worship, to preach and to have some conversation with a large number of people. Saturdays are often busy, with weddings and various social and community occasions at which we will need to be present. One weekday should be kept as a day off. The other four weekdays should be divided into three sections: the morning, the afternoon and the evening. We were told that we should aim to work two out of the three parts of the day, and the third part should be for leisure, family, friends, exercise or recreation. The morning should always, if possible, be spent in the study. This was the time for prayer, reading the Bible, commentary work, reading, letters and sermon preparation. The afternoon or evening were for being out in the parish; for pastoral visiting, the youth club, the church council and other meetings and events.

I have to say that this is a model that I have never been able to apply consistently to my own life in any strict or disciplined way. However, it has given me a clear sense of the appropriate balance that I should be aiming at in my own use of time. I have also known other ministers who have been able to implement this model of life in ministry. A leading evangelical clergyman in Cambridge during my own time there was known simply to be unavailable for church leaders' meetings on weekday mornings. He spent his morning in his study, in the way that our principal at Wycliffe Hall, Oxford, had set out for us. The church where this man was the vicar was widely known for the quality of its expository biblical preaching and teaching, and the church grew steadily year after year during his time there. I have no doubt that this is a model of life in ministry which works, if only we are able to follow it and to resist the inevitable pressure to be available for meetings.

Control of the diary

The diary is a wonderful tool which we can use to set out and maintain our priorities for the use of our time. Sometimes there will be urgent and unavoidable events and situations that will take precedence over whatever we have planned. The diary, well utililsed, can enable us to organise the use of our time and can help us to ensure that our planning does not simply remain in the realm of good intentions.

If we want to take a monthly Quiet Day, we should put it in the diary. If we plan to spend a significant amount of time each week in prayer, reading, reflection and sermon preparation, we need to keep that time clear in the diary. Otherwise, the danger is, for example, that preparation for the Sunday sermon will be squeezed out until Saturday afternoon or evening. If this becomes a regular pattern, our preaching is likely to be shallow and insubstantial, and the effectiveness of our ministry will be compromised.

Our diaries are a telling revelation of our actual priorities. What we do is far more important than what we say about ourselves. If we are wise, we will face these realities and listen to what they are telling us. This is the task of self-management, and it is probably the toughest management task that any of us have to face.

The key is to prioritise, to make the right decisions about what is truly important and of lasting significance for us and for the work to which we have been called. The diary can help us to avoid the tyranny of the urgent. It can enable us to plan our use of time, almost like an athlete's training schedule, to enable us to become more and more what God is calling us to be.

The diary can also give us a sense of permission to spend time on activities that may otherwise seem difficult to justify to our congregation. Eugene Peterson has written a number of excellent books on the spirituality of pastoral ministry. In his book entitled *Under the Predictable Plant: An exploration in vocational holiness* Peterson describes a time in his own ministry when he was going through something of a crisis and needed help. He tried to find a mentor or guide to help him work out his vocation in a difficult place. Then, Peterson says, he found Fyodor Dostoevsky. 'I took my appointments calendar and wrote in two-hour meetings with "FD" three afternoons a week. Over the next seven months I read through the entire corpus, some of it twice. From three to five o'clock on Tuesday, Thursday, and Friday I met with FD in my study and had leisurely conversations through *Crime and Punishment, Letters from the Underworld, The Idiot, A Raw Youth, The Devils, The Brothers Karamazov*. I spent those afternoons with a man for whom God and passion were integral—and integrated. And then the crisis was over.'[14]

Sharing the ministry

A central principle of contemplative ministry is that we do not attempt to do all the ministry ourselves. I aim to concentrate on the calling that God has given to me, and I trust that he will call and draw in others with different gifts for all the other work which needs to be done. I remember a time during my first parish appointment when the rector of the church decided for a short while to change the way in which the pew leaflet described the team of ministers. The first line was revised to read, 'Ministers: All the members of the congregation'. After this the rector, curate, youth leader, administrator and other team members were listed by name.

It is very difficult to develop a model of contemplative ministry unless there is an understanding of shared ministry among the leaders and the congregation. We all have different gifts and strengths, and a healthy church is one in which every member is enabled to play their part. For myself as leader this requires a willingness to make space for others to offer their gifts, and sometimes to do things differently to the way I would have done them.

A few years ago the then Bishop of Salisbury, David Stancliffe, met with a group of women and men whom he was preparing to ordain the following day in Salisbury Cathedral. Bishop David said to them that he would be ordaining them to find what is life-giving and to do it. He said, 'If you are being asked to do something and it's not life-giving to you, then perhaps someone else will want to do it. If you don't want to do it and no one else wants to do it, then you can probably let it go.'

Of course there will always be tasks that we have to do even though we would prefer not to. That is the nature of sacrificial service; it is often costly and difficult, but it is part of what is involved in obedience to Christ. However, this does not mean that our best energies should be consumed week after week in tasks and chores that are not what we were called or ordained to do. Many clergy see stretching out before them an endless grind of church building maintenance, fundraising and village fetes, meetings and more meetings. Add to this a week that now involves five funerals, a simmering conflict with the choir master over the choice of hymns, and a visit from the finance committee to find out why the church income declined last year. These are the realities of parish ministry for many ordained ministers. It is not surprising that many may start to say, 'Surely this is not what I was ordained to do. Is this really what the service of the kingdom of God amounts to?'

As we become more experienced in ministry, we are likely to discover that, if we are to be faithful to our vocation, we will have to make some tough choices. We will have to accept that there are some tasks that need to be done, but we will not be able to do them. There are some things we will have to do for a short while, until we can find someone else to take over. But we must hold firm to the vision of what we have been called by God to be and to do, and to trust God that he will call and draw in people to do the tasks that we cannot—or should not—do.

Some members of our congregation may not find this easy to understand and accept. We have to be willing to take some time over this, as we explain to our leaders and congregation what we see as our first calling, and why it is important that we are faithful to the role of spiritual leader, teacher and pastor. We can explain that this will mean that we cannot do everything, and that we are seeking to be faithful to the biblical view of the Church as the body of Christ with many members and many varieties of gifts (1 Corinthians 12). As we teach and live this model of ministry, we will find that many people will increasingly recognise the effectiveness and importance of what we are trying to do, particularly as a greater fruitfulness becomes apparent in the spirituality and service of the Church.

Being a contemplative minister means not attempting to be someone who does everything in the life of the Church. We let go, we delegate, and we concentrate on the key tasks which belong to the role of spiritual leader and pastor. Of course we will face various different expectations of what the minister or vicar should do. There is no way that we can meet everyone's expectations. So we must ask, again and again, 'What has God called me to be and to do?' If we are clear about our first call, the call to love God and to walk daily in relationship with him, then we will be enabled to make the other choices that come to us. We are not called to try to do everything or to please everybody.

We all need to give our best energy and time to the following of our true vocation. David Stancliffe is right—it is all about life. We have to find what is life-giving for us and for those whom we serve. We make that our first call, our priority in the use of our time. What will lead us and our people into a deeper relationship with God? What will enable the Church to grow and flourish, to be a community that is full of life and joy and care for others? That is what pastoral ministry is really all about. That is what we should be about.

Part Three

Prayer

Chapter 4

Living from
the still centre

O God, forasmuch as without thee we are not able to please thee;
Mercifully grant that thy Holy Spirit may in all things direct and
rule our hearts; through Jesus Christ our Lord. Amen
THE COLLECT: THE NINETEENTH SUNDAY AFTER TRINITY,
THE BOOK OF COMMON PRAYER

WHAT IS PRAYER? If the first call of those in ministry is to be men and women of prayer, and to teach others to pray, what does this mean?

Prayer can mean many different things to different people. A school motto that I came across in South Africa declared in Latin: *laborare est orare* —To work is to pray. I did not find this understanding of prayer helpful. It seemed to me to be saying that work is the same as prayer, and that the harder you work, the more you will be praying. I now understand that the Benedictine view of life is centred on a balance between prayer, work and study, and that all of these are seen to be vital in the development of our relationship with God. Prayer and work go together, and the Benedictine rule of life has much to offer those seeking a way of living which can draw them closer to God in today's culture.

I have increasingly come to see prayer as not so much something I do when I make specific times to pray, but as relationship with God, encompassing the whole of life. Specific times which are set aside for prayer are important, but they are only part of what constitutes a life of prayer. To be a person of prayer means living a life of being close to God, of being drawn into an intimate union with God. The challenge for me over many years has been to take the closeness to God which I have experienced in prayer and worship, and to live my whole life in this deeper reality.

This has been brought home to me on a number of occasions when I have been away for a silent retreat, beginning on a Monday evening and ending on a Friday morning. During the time of retreat I have been living in a simplified and stable world of silence, prayer, rest, reading and good food, for three days and four nights. Many of these retreats have been for me rich and profound times of drawing close to God, although there have been some where I have found the silence hard and have known myself to be going through times of struggle and pain. Often, by the end of a retreat, I have come away with a renewed determination to live my life as though it were all a retreat. I have longed to simplify and structure my daily life in order that I may stay in a place of intimacy with God.

In other words, the desire of my heart has been to be so deeply rooted in God, in silence and simplicity, that I would be able to respond to each encounter and experience of daily life from these same depths of silent wonder. This seems to me to be what the religious or monastic life seeks to enable, this ordered and contained world which draws the heart to be set upon God in all of daily life.

The problem, I discovered, is that the reality of life makes this very difficult. After a four-day retreat I could usually manage a day or two when my heart continued to be tuned in to the depth and silence of the retreat, but after that it was back to normal. I would be swept along by the endless demands and activity of my normal life, and the reactions and responses that these evoked in me. So the longing remained within me, largely unrealised and unfulfilled. How do I live my daily life from a still centre? Is it even possible?

At one point I spent ten months doing the 'Ignatian Spiritual Exercises in Daily Life' with a member of a religious community in Cambridge. I met with her once a week and wrote many pages of reflection on my prayer journey through the Ignatian Exercises. My goal in all of this was that God would show me how I could be close to him in the midst of a busy life. What I learnt from all this was not so much how to live a quiet and peaceful life, but that there were forces and motivations within me that were driving me on in the relentless busyness of my life. Until I came to terms with these drivers and compulsions, there would be no simple solution to my longings.

Living from the still centre in the midst of a busy life is not the same as being away on a silent retreat in a beautiful part of England. The reality of life is that there are times when I am in good shape, when life is great and I feel well and in control. The problem for me is that there are other times, when I don't feel good and I am definitely not in control. The truth, I have come to realise, is that I am in fact close to God when I am weak and not in control. I have come to realise that I need a spirituality that embraces all of these realities. Living from the still centre is not dependent on outward circumstances. It is rather the inner truth of my relationship with God in Christ. This is what holds me firm regardless of what life brings.

The Psalms are often described as being the prayer book of the Bible. There are many different kinds of psalm. There are the 'nice' ones, such as Psalm 23, assuring us that the Lord is our shepherd, and that goodness and mercy will follow us all the days of our lives. Then there are the psalms that make for uncomfortable reading. Psalm 44 is one example. 'Where are you, Lord? What's going on? Wake up, Lord. Have you gone to sleep?' This may be a strange kind of prayer to our ears, but there is a truthfulness here that speaks of what life is really like at times. It seems to me significant that the psalmist is still speaking to God, even though his prayers are full of anger and pain.

The eminent theologian Walter Brueggemann has written about the spirituality of the Psalms, and he describes three categories of psalm. There are psalms of orientation, psalms of disorientation and psalms of new orientation. Brueggemann says that 'human life consists in satisfied seasons of well-being that evoke gratitude for the constancy of blessing'. This is reflected in the psalms of orientation. Then there are other seasons: '... anguished seasons of hurt, alienation, suffering and death'. Matching this are the psalms of disorientation. Thirdly, 'human life consists in turns of surprise when we are overwhelmed with the new gifts of God, when joy breaks through the despair'.[15] These are the times of new orientation.

What the psalms are saying to the Church is that this is what life is like, and this is the reality that should be reflected in our praying, because true prayer embraces all that life brings. Our God is not only the God of the good times when we are well and comfortable and in control. He is the God of the difficult times, and indeed he shows himself to us in new and significant ways when we are weak and hungry, thirsty and desperate. We need a way of praying that enables us to bring the whole of our experience of life to God, and not just the 'nice' bits, the presentable bits, the happy bits.

Prayer is the place in our inner being where we deal with the reality of all that life throws at us, and with the reality of our own human nature. The fact is that none of us finds this easy or straightforward. There is a battle that we fight every day to live in the place of prayer. Our first instinct in most of the daily situations that we face is to take care of the self. I turn first of all to my need and desire for self-preservation and self-promotion. 'How am I going to deal with this? How will this affect me, or reflect upon me?' This is usually my immediate response to most of what happens to me.

I can start the day in quietness and prayer, but soon there are issues to deal with. I drive to work, and the other drivers are racing past and cutting in, and I am trying, often unsuccessfully, not to react. There are complex pastoral issues to deal with, and pressure to meet deadlines and to produce results. And then machines break down and computers malfunction, and then I feel ill with a stomach upset. It's not easy staying close to God when all of this is going on.

It doesn't take long before my idealised peaceful and sanctified state of being is gone. I feel that I am being pulled in a hundred different directions, and God has withdrawn to the sidelines, as I plough on as best I can. I know in my heart that God is not simply watching from a distance, but that is nonetheless how it often feels.

What I am finding is that the answer, the remedy, is contemplative prayer. This does not mean that life becomes any easier; in fact the difficulties of life continue and if anything intensify. Contemplative prayer is the still centre, the place of being in God's presence, in wordless waiting, and of experiencing the peace that passes understanding. This is the daily practice that changes our hearts, that holds us and guards us through all the events and challenges of life. Through contemplative prayer we become more and more attuned to the place of inner silence, where God can be God, and we are his beloved.

It does not seem to me that God has called me to live a quiet and simple life, because life as a pastor is not simple, and often we are required to be busy. There are many difficulties and many struggles along the way. There are also many joys and the work is often deeply rewarding. This is the life and ministry to which I have been called. But God has also called me to be rooted in his love and his unfailing presence through all that life brings, which is why I need a daily discipline of contemplative praying.

Most religious communities insist on a discipline of regular times of prayer and worship through the day, some silent and some corporate. This is because they know that it is very difficult to stay centred on God unless we regularly return to the place of prayer, of ceasing from activity and becoming still. We need this because in the rush and the demands of everyday life we all find ourselves responding not from a still centre but from the self, the 'me' that is always there, needing to be reassured or protected or defended. In coming back to the still centre I am able to let go of the pride and the self-concern that has come to the fore in the past hours, and to meet again the grace and unconditional love of the Father, who accepts me as I truly am.

In the Diocese of Salisbury I have been privileged to share the leadership of our 'Contemplative Minister' days with Sue Langdon. Sue is a contemplative priest who lives alone in a remote village in west Dorset, and she is a highly sought-after spiritual guide and companion to many people engaged in parish ministry. Sue often says to the groups that we lead,

'If you remember only three words from this day, these are the words that are supremely important: compassion, compassion, compassion. You can forget everything else that we have said, as long as you remember this.' It is of crucial importance in all of this that we have compassion for ourselves.

It is all too easy to be hard on ourselves, to feel unworthy and condemned, because again and again we fail to live as we have intended. We know that we are called to live a life of prayer, of being and behaving as we are called by God to be and to do. But the world is all around us, and the pull of the 'me first' self is very strong. We cannot dare to forget that our God is full of compassion, and his mercy is everlasting. He knows us and he loves us as we are. 'He knows how we were made' (Psalm 103:14), and he looks upon us with unfailing love and compassion.

'The Lord is merciful and gracious, slow to anger and abounding in steadfast love.... As a father has compassion for his children, so the Lord has compassion for those who fear him' (Psalm 103:8, 13).

As Richard Rohr says, 'God leads by compassion toward the soul, never by condemnation.'[16] So easily I find that I can turn to judging, to condemnation, because other people do not meet my standards or expectations, and I myself do not meet them either. In a sense I fail constantly, but that is not the final word. The final word is that in Christ I am set free from condemnation, and I live in mercy and in freedom. 'There is therefore now no condemnation for those who are in Christ Jesus. For the law of the Spirit of life in Christ Jesus has set you free from the law of sin and death' (Romans 8:1–2). We also read in John that 'if the Son makes you free, you will be free indeed' (John 8:36).

There is a great truth here. We are not to return to law and to slavery, especially the slavery of the false self, but we are made for freedom in Christ. The life of prayer is the life of the heart, of the still centre which is held by the unfailing love and mercy of God. Christ gives us the gift of his peace, which the world cannot give. This is not something we can earn; it is his gift to us. But we must receive his peace, and this requires that we cease from our striving and our self-preoccupation, and be still. When we abide in the peace of Christ, then we are living the life of prayer, the life of the still centre.

Chapter 5

The life of prayer

O Lord, we beseech thee mercifully to receive the prayers of thy people which call upon thee; and grant that they may both perceive and know what things they ought to do, and also may have grace and power faithfully to fulfil the same; through Jesus Christ our Lord. Amen

THE COLLECT: THE FIRST SUNDAY AFTER THE EPIPHANY,
THE BOOK OF COMMON PRAYER

Let the words of my mouth and the meditation of my heart be acceptable to you, O Lord, my rock and my redeemer.

PSALM 19:14

A LIFE OF PRAYER is a life rooted in relationship with God, where our intention is that the meditations of our hearts are always pleasing to him. Evagrius Ponticus says that 'prayer is the intimate conversation of the mind [or spirit] with God'.[17]

Evagrius Ponticus was born in 364 in Ibora Pontus in Cappadocia in what is now Turkey. He studied rhetoric in Constantinople, where he was ordained priest by Gregory Nazianzus. He then fell in love with a married woman and fled to Jerusalem, and later made his way to the desert of Nitria, where he died in 399. His writings on prayer have a clarity and power which is in keeping with the teaching and wisdom of the Desert Fathers. For Evagrius, Christian prayer is the continual conversation of the spirit with God.

Being a person of prayer is a way of life; it is not simply a matter of a few religious habits or disciplines. Sr. Pascale-Dominque Nau writes, 'In the purest tradition of the Desert Fathers, Evagrius shows that life and prayer are one: they are mutually supportive and flourish harmoniously together. Prayer is not just an intellectual activity; it involves the whole person: body, memory, intelligence and heart.'[18] As I have read and studied Evagrius' *Chapters on Prayer*, I have found that his teaching from some 1600 years ago has brought new insight to my own understanding of the life of prayer in the 21st century.

With some reference to the writings of Evagrius Ponticus, I have reflected on how I experience a life of prayer. What helps me to pray? This is not about theory or idealism. This is an honest and practical reflection on what seems to me to be helpful in drawing me to an intimate conversation of the mind and heart with God in daily life. We are all different, and so for some there will be other things that are important or helpful. It seems that a good place to start is with this question: what helps me to pray?

Discipline

We must make daily time or times to be still and draw near to God. This involves a determination of our will. Unless we find the time to do this, the time will not find us. If the desire of my heart is to be a person of prayer, I must act upon this like an athlete training for a marathon. I may have an ambition to run the London Marathon, but unless I start a proper training programme and persevere with it, this is not going to happen. I have to move beyond pensive longing and mere words. If I have a serious intention of living the life of prayer, this will mean spending time each day alone with God, as a normal pattern of life.

Silence and stillness

Contemplative prayer is the prayer of the heart. The Russian mystic Theophan the Recluse says, 'To pray is to descend with the mind into the heart, and there to stand before the face of the Lord, ever-present, all-seeing within you.'[19] Jesus says, 'Blessed are the pure in heart, for they will see God' (Matthew 5:8).

So much of our lives seems to be lived in our heads, in the endless analysing and rationalising and replaying of the events and responses that make up our lives. We are a cerebral culture; we believe that we can think our way to the solution to all our problems. Many of us are starting to realise that maybe we think too much. Through the practice of contemplative prayer we learn to move from the head to the heart, and to be still before God. There are a number of ways in which we can do this, and different teachings and practices have been helpful to different people. It is important that you choose a particular teaching or discipline which works for you, rather than adopting a 'pick and mix' approach. The teachings of Christian meditation and the Jesus Prayer are widely used, and in our diocese we have found the practice of Centring Prayer as taught by Thomas Keating and Cynthia Bourgeault has been helpful to many. Essentially the practice is as follows.

Take up a position where, as far as possible, your muscles don't have to do any work. Sit upright with your feet resting on the ground, and breathe more slowly and deeply. Aim for a child's relaxation, not straining or tense. The present contains the everyday sounds and the passing thoughts, but we simply let them go. The dog walks past, a telephone rings, but we let it go. We aim to sustain a quality of awareness and stillness and attention. This is more important than the quantity of prayer. Remember that worship and prayer are part of rest, because our need above all is to be spiritually restored (see Matthew 11:28).

Come before God and begin with the Lord's Prayer, or an appropriate verse of scripture, with your full attention. Have a definite place and time, and try to keep to it. A word or phrase can help us, when distracted, to return to our primary intention of being still before God; for example, 'Abba Father', 'peace' or 'Lord have mercy'. We may choose to focus on an object: a leaf, a chalice, a candle, a cross. Don't start preaching a sermon to yourself or moralising.

The journey inwards is the object of this kind of prayer. We live outwards so much. Our identity seems to consist of the parts we play in different circumstances. We try to succeed in doing this well, but this is not our true self. We are often so concerned with the impression we are making and, much of the time, we are performers. In the place of being still before God, our hearts become deeply open to him. By his Spirit we are drawn closer to Christ's heart of love, where we are set free to become our true selves.

Simplicity

It is good to begin clearing the clutter and noise that crowds in upon our hearts. A life of simplicity is the natural response to purity of heart. As we are drawn into this quality of living, we will want to take action against the pressures and demands of consumerism and the information age. I have often noticed how those who live in communities with prayer at the centre will create a peaceful and uncluttered environment: a place of peace with simple, good, nutritious food and plenty of quiet.

As we seek to live the life of prayer, we too will want to clear some of the clutter from our lives and the spaces we inhabit. This is a satisfying and joy-giving task. It's good to be simple and it's good to be free.

Awareness of God

Many of us find that it is helpful, if not essential, to find or to create a place where our attention is drawn to an awareness of God. For me, being alone in a quiet place where I can look at the countryside, at the natural world, has always been important. I love to go into the New Forest, near to where I live, and just sit in the car, listen to the birds, and wait on God. In previous parishes I have found other places which have become special to me as places to be alone with God: beside the River Cam just north of Cambridge, and in the Holme Fen reserve, a beautiful forested nature reserve deep in the Cambridgeshire Fens. If we are seeking to know the presence of God, we should begin not with the invisible and the abstract, but with what we can see before us, and with what God has made. To gaze at the beauty of the natural world can quickly lead our hearts to an awareness of God and of his goodness and his peace.

Equally, we may set aside a room or a particular chair in our homes as a place where we can sit and gaze and be still. Often it is good to have an icon or picture, or perhaps a candle, to focus our attention. I have a large block-mounted copy of Rublev's icon in my study, which draws my heart to the infinite and mysterious love of my triune God, the ceaseless love which enfolds me, no matter what state my heart is in. Ideally, we will find a place where there are few or no distractions, where we will not be easily disturbed by telephone calls, by other people's conversations or questions, or by our own unfinished tasks and concerns.

Repentance and forgiveness

Each day, morning and evening, we return to the Lord, confessing our sin and receiving the assurance that we are made new in Christ. 'Therefore, since we are justified by faith, we have peace with God through our Lord Jesus Christ' (Romans 5:1).

The wisdom of the daily offices of the Church of morning and evening prayer gives us a simple prayer of repentance and the assurance of God's mercy and forgiveness. This is necessary because the 'me first' self is always up to its tricks, and inevitably it leaves its debris behind it, in our lives and in the lives of those around us. Somehow in the church today, repentance seems to have become unfashionable. As we grow in our love for God, surely we will also feel more deeply a sorrow for our own falling short of his heart of love and care for all his creation. Without repentance and forgiveness we will not be able to keep our hearts in the place of peace with God. Evagrius Ponticus says, 'If you have the impression that in your prayer you no longer need to shed tears for your sins, consider how far you have moved away from God, despite the fact that you should always be with him. Then you will shed hot tears.'[20]

Scripture

The practice of contemplative prayer should go hand in hand with the daily reading and study of the Bible, and especially the Psalms and the Gospels. I have found great value in the practice of *lectio divina*, in which we read the words of the Bible and listen to what the Spirit of God is saying to us through his word before us, and then wait on him for the opening of new faith and truth to our hearts. We ask, 'What are you saying to me today, Lord? What is your word to me through this passage of scripture?' We wait and we listen. We let go of our own agendas and we open ourselves to whatever God may want to say to us today.

What seems important to me is not the amount or the length of the passages that we read, but a few words taken in deeply and sometimes memorised. It can be helpful to memorise those parts of the Bible that have particular meaning or resonance for us, and to which we can come back again and again, such as the Magnificat or Psalm 23.

Perseverance

The life of prayer is a life of ever deepening trust in God, regardless of the circumstances. We learn perseverance as our faith and our intention is put to the test. All of this throws us more and more upon God, and on our trust in his unfailing love and his promises to us. Thomas Merton said, 'The whole Christian life is a life in which the further a person progresses, the more he or she has to depend directly on God. The more we progress, the less we are self-sufficient. The more we progress, the poorer we get so that the person who has progressed the most is totally poor and depends directly on God.'[21]

Like an athlete in training we will have to learn to endure pain and to overcome obstacles if we are to finish the race. Evagrius Ponticus says, 'Don't refuse to be poor and tried by tribulations; they are the fuel that makes prayer easy.'[22]

He also says, 'Don't grieve, if God doesn't immediately give you what you have asked Him, for He wants to do more good by your perseverance in His presence in prayer (Romans 12:12). Indeed what is greater than to converse with God and being drawn into an intimate union with Him?'[23]

Resist the enemy

Prayer is a battle in which we will have to fight. There is much that will try to prevent us from coming to the place of prayer and of silence. Sometimes that old 'me first' self will find every way possible to distract us and to persuade us that we are not able right now to take time to be still and rest before God. We will become aware of an inner struggle, a wrestling, and a battle which we may sometimes not immediately win, because we find other things to do, or some reason not to go to the place of prayer.

The truth is that contemplative prayer is profoundly transformational. Through this practice our hearts become pure in God's sight, and we find being formed in us, day by day, the true self that God has created each of us to be. So it's not surprising that the false self on which we have relied for many years will find this hard. The deep inner change that is taking place as we establish ourselves in the practice of contemplative prayer will result in struggle. The old self is so used to trying to cope, to protect and defend us, to bolster our self-sufficiency, and it is not easy to let go of these long-held patterns as we are drawn, slowly but surely, into utter dependence on God for our security and our needs.

True prayer is the deepest and most profound work of God in the human heart, and it is a spiritual battle. Paul says in Ephesians 6:12–13, 'For our struggle is not against enemies of blood and flesh, but against the rulers, against the authorities, against the cosmic powers of this present darkness, against the spiritual forces of evil in the heavenly places. Therefore take up the whole armour of God, so that you may be able to withstand on that evil day, and having done everything, to stand firm.' We must never forget or disregard the seriousness and intensity of the battle that is involved for all those who commit themselves wholeheartedly to the life of prayer.

Holy Communion

The body and blood of Jesus is our spiritual food and drink. In John 6:53 Jesus says, 'Very truly, I tell you, unless you eat the flesh of the Son of Man and drink his blood, you have no life in you.' If we are to abide in Christ we must regularly share in his body and blood through Holy Communion.

When I was 13 years old I was confirmed into the Anglican Church in Natal in South Africa, and was able to receive Holy Communion. I was at boarding school where Sunday church attendance was compulsory, but being confirmed meant that I could go to the 7 am service of Holy Communion at the local parish church, and then I would not have to attend the evening service at St George's Garrison Church together with all the other boarders. I soon found that, although I had little real idea of what being a Christian meant, I knew in some mysterious way that I met God at the Communion rail. In receiving the bread and wine in Holy Communion I experienced the cleansing of my sin and an unmistakeable sense of the peace which passes understanding. This I now see as being a key stage in the process that led to my later growth into a serious and lifelong commitment to following Jesus Christ.

What helps me to live the life of prayer? This is not some vague or mysterious goal, or a longing somehow to become a mystic one day. It is relatively simple and practical. For me, it means discipline, silence and stillness, simplicity, cultivating an awareness of God, daily repentance and forgiveness, scripture, perseverance, and regularly receiving Holy Communion. Underlying all of this is the grace of God in Christ Jesus, and my need each day for the help, guidance and presence of the Holy Spirit. We do not enter this way of living on our own. We are part of the great communion of saints who offer up unceasing prayer to God. In all of this we are led by the Spirit of truth, the helper and comforter promised to all his disciples by Jesus.

Part Four

Rooted in Jesus

Chapter 6

Being led by the Spirit

God, who on this day didst teach the hearts of thy faithful people,
by the sending to them the light of thy Holy Spirit; Grant us by the
same Spirit to have a right judgement in all things, and evermore
to rejoice in his holy comfort; through the merits of Christ Jesus
our Saviour, who liveth and reigneth with thee, in the unity of the
same Spirit, one God, world without end. Amen

THE COLLECT FOR WHITSUNDAY, THE BOOK OF COMMON PRAYER

Now the Lord is the Spirit, and where the Spirit of the Lord is, there
is freedom. And all of us, with unveiled faces, seeing the glory of
the Lord as though reflected in a mirror, are being transformed
into the same image from one degree of glory to another; for this
comes from the Lord, the Spirit.

2 CORINTHIANS 3:17–18

AS A PRIEST in the Anglican Church, a prayer that I have used in public worship probably more than any other, apart from the Lord's Prayer, is this: 'The peace of God, which passes all understanding, keep your hearts and minds in the knowledge and love of God, and of his Son Jesus Christ our Lord; and the blessing of God Almighty, the Father, the Son, and the Holy Spirit, be among you and remain with you always' (based on Philippians 4:7).

Like with many prayers, it is easy to say these words and become very familiar with them, without recognising much of the meaning that lies behind them. What, for example, is the peace which 'passes all understanding'? In a culture where rational understanding and analysis is the key to almost all that we do in daily life, this is something that we may struggle to grasp and accept. Can there even be a peace that passes all human understanding?

This prayer is invoking the peace of God, which is able to keep our hearts and minds in the knowledge and love of God and of his Son Jesus Christ our Lord. This means that, if we have this peace, we will be enabled to live a life of prayer, of intimate conversation of the mind and heart with God. From this will flow into our lives the blessing of God, Father, Son and Holy Spirit.

The peace of God which passes all understanding is the peace which Jesus promised in John 14:27: 'Peace I leave with you; my peace I give to you. I do not give to you as the world gives. Do not let your hearts be troubled, and do not let them be afraid.' This peace is given us by the promised Holy Spirit, the Advocate or Comforter promised by Jesus to those who follow him. As the Gospel verse says, it is not 'peace as the world gives'. This is not a matter of the absence of conflict or noise or stress. In fact, it is peace in the very midst of conflict and stress.

The life of being led by the Spirit is, first of all, about allowing the Holy Spirit to dwell and to rule in our hearts. In Colossians 3:15 Paul writes, 'Let the peace of Christ rule in your hearts, to which indeed you were called in the one body. And be thankful.' Again, we see here the importance of the biblical understanding of the heart as key to so much of the life of knowing and serving God.

Cruden's Complete Concordance says, 'The word heart is used in Scripture as the seat of life or strength; hence it means mind, soul, spirit, or one's entire emotional nature and understanding. It is also used as the centre or inner part of a thing.'[24] Henri Nouwen writes in his book *The Way of the Heart*, 'In our milieu the word heart has become a soft word. It refers to the seat of the sentimental life... But the word heart in the Jewish-Christian tradition refers to the source of all physical, emotional, intellectual, volitional, and moral energies.'[25]

The fruit of the Holy Spirit is the outflowing of what is in our hearts. Being led by the Holy Spirit means that our hearts will be changed, and that more and more we will be enabled to live holy lives, lives of love and peace and joy (Galatians 5:22). This will be the practical outworking of hearts that are ruled by the love of God and the peace of Christ.

The Holy Spirit cleanses the thoughts of our hearts

At the beginning of the Anglican service of Holy Communion we pray: 'Almighty God, to whom all hearts are open, all desires known and from whom no secrets are hidden: cleanse the thoughts of our hearts by the inspiration of your Holy Spirit, that we may perfectly love you, and worthily magnify your holy name; through Christ our Lord.'[26]

The work of the Holy Spirit is to cleanse the thoughts of our hearts. The peace which passes all understanding comes from hearts that are cleansed and reconciled to God in Christ Jesus. Paul says, 'So if anyone is in Christ, there is a new creation: everything old has passed away; see, everything has become new! All this is from God, who reconciled himself to us through Christ, and has given us the ministry of reconciliation' (2 Corinthians 5:17–18).

It is through turning from all that is not pleasing to God and his heart of love, and through trusting in the redeeming work of Jesus, that we have peace with God, and we are reconciled or made right with him. Daily we fall short; daily we sin; daily we need to return to the One whose love is constant and unfailing. The service of Holy Communion provides an extraordinary opportunity, given to us by Jesus himself, for this returning and reconciling to take place, again and again.

The Holy Spirit fills our hearts with the assurance of God's love

The Holy Spirit is given by Jesus to be our Comforter. The Greek word used here in the Gospel is the word *parakletos,* which literally means someone called alongside to help. Hence it may be translated 'advocate' or simply 'helper'. The Holy Spirit is given to fill our hearts with a deep assurance of God's unfailing love for us, in all that happens to us in our daily lives.

The word 'comforter' also enables us to see the Holy Spirit as the person of the Holy Trinity who dwells or abides in us in order that we may be set free from fear and anxiety. The Comforter is not sent by Jesus to make his people comfortable. He is sent to give us the peace which passes all understanding, so that our hearts are not anxious, troubled or afraid. This is what Jesus promised (see John 14:27). This is said immediately after Jesus has assured the disciples that, although he will no longer be physically with them, the Father will send the Comforter in his name to enable them to live as he has taught them. 'You know him,' says Jesus, 'because he abides with you and will be in you' (v. 17).

The comfort the Holy Spirit brings will sometimes in reality be quite uncomfortable for us. This is a comfort intended to strengthen us to live and minister boldly and courageously in Christ's service. David Watson describes in his book *One in the Spirit* how the meaning of the word comfort has changed. Watson writes, 'Do not be deceived by the Authorised Version's "Comforter". The original meaning of "Comforter" is something very different from what we imagine today. In the famous Bayeux tapestry, King William is seen with a sword prodding one of his soldiers into battle. Underneath is this caption: "King William comforteth his soldiers."!'[27]

The Holy Spirit leads us into the truth of who we are in Christ

The Holy Spirit enables us to be courageous in living faithfully as followers of Jesus. The fact is that life is often hard. Bob Dylan in his autobiographical book, *Chronicles Volume One* writes about his grandma who lived with the family when Bob was growing up in a small town in Minnesota. He says, 'She was filled with nobility and goodness, told me once that happiness isn't on the road to anything. That happiness is the road. Had also instructed me to be kind because everyone you'll ever meet is fighting a hard battle.'[28]

It takes courage and faith to live each day and live it well. The Christian life is a life of faith. Paul says, 'We walk by faith and not by sight' (2 Corinthians 5:7). Where does this faith and courage come from? At its deepest level, faith is a deep trust and sense of being utterly secure in God's care and love. The Holy Spirit is the one who enables us to know in our hearts the truth of who we are in Christ. Our deepest identity is that we are beloved of God, in and through his Son Jesus

Christ. The Spirit of truth anchors my heart in the truth of God's salvation and his eternal and unfailing love for me. This is my deepest identity, my true security, my true self in God, from which all true faith and trust will spring.

Chapter 7

Finding our rootedness in Christ

IN THE EARLY 1980s I was working in a parish in Sheffield, doing a second curacy, and at the same time completing an MA in Biblical Studies and Hermeneutics at Sheffield University. During this time our son John was born, our first child. It was an extraordinary and special time in our lives. Before long the vicar raised the question of the baptism. At the time I was thinking that the biblical norm was that some acknowledgement of personal faith should be present at baptism. My feeling was that I would prefer my son to be dedicated as an infant, and then baptised later when he was old enough to know what was happening. However, I wasn't sure, and I needed to be more clear about the biblical basis for infant baptism.

I wrestled with this as part of my studies in the interpretation and authority of the Bible at Sheffield University. In this I was greatly helped by one of my teachers, Dr Tony Thiselton, to whom I owe a great deal. He helped me to see that at the heart of this issue is the question of what it means to be 'in Christ Jesus'. This is a phrase which is repeated many times in the New Testament. It is central to Paul's understanding of what it means to be Christian. Our deepest identity is that we are 'in Christ' (see Romans 8:1–3; 2 Corinthians 5:17; Ephesians 3:21; Philippians 3:3).

This is a huge subject, and I could write a few chapters on this alone. At the time that we were in Sheffield it was particularly significant because I realised that if someone is 'in Christ Jesus', then it is appropriate and right that they should be baptised. Is it possible that an infant Christian child can be 'in Christ Jesus'? I came to believe that in a Christian family in the household of faith, this was entirely appropriate. My wife Alison and I believed that our son had been born into the new covenant community of faith in Christ. Our prayer and commitment was that he would grow up in that community, and that his whole life from the moment of his birth would be 'in Christ Jesus'. So we decided to go ahead with the baptism, and we are still clear to this day that this was the right decision.

Our deepest identity and security as Christians is 'in Christ Jesus'. This is who we truly are before God, our true selves, clothed in the grace, mercy and love of Jesus. This is therefore how we should seek to live as Christians, as the daughters and sons of God in Christ. It is all about the love of God enfolding and embracing us, and making us new creations in Christ.

As time has passed, I have continued to develop my understanding and awareness of this important phrase 'in Christ'. What does it mean for me to be 'in Christ'? It seems to me to be the basis for my understanding of the transforming work of God in my life. God is working constantly by his Spirit to change us into the likeness of Christ. Sometimes we respond well to his work in us; sometimes we try hard to hold on to our old ways. Spiritual formation has been described as the process of being conformed to the image of Christ for the sake of others. Paul says, 'Now the Lord is the Spirit, and where the Spirit of the Lord is, there is freedom. And all of us, with unveiled faces, seeing the glory of the Lord as though reflected in a mirror, are being transformed into the same image from one degree of glory to another; for this comes from the Lord, the Spirit' (2 Corinthians 3:17–18). It is the work of the Holy Spirit to bring about this transformation in us.

Being transformed into Christ

The problem for us is the cost involved in order for this change to take place. The old false self which is always trying to defend me and promote my interests and my reputation has to go through a refining fire, so that Christ may be formed in me. Paul spells this out in 2 Corinthians 4. In verse 5 he says, 'For we do not proclaim ourselves; we proclaim Jesus Christ as Lord and ourselves as your slaves for Jesus' sake.' How is it that we come to proclaim in our ministry not ourselves and our own egos and ambitions and insecurities, but Jesus Christ as Lord and ourselves as servants or slaves for the sake of Jesus? Paul tells us in verses 7–12. He speaks about being 'afflicted in every way, but not crushed; perplexed, but not driven to despair; persecuted, but not forsaken; struck down, but not destroyed; always carrying in the body the death of Jesus, so that the life of Jesus may also be made visible in our bodies' (vv. 8–10). In other words, transformation is costly. This is not about just rearranging a few things on the circumference of our lives, or adopting a few religious habits like giving up chocolates or television for Lent. This not what Paul is describing here. It is about hard battles, costing no less than everything.

Sometimes I have found ministry and Church leadership very tough. When you are bleeding and wounded, and all you want to do is step back from the fight for a while, to sit down somewhere and rest and have someone tend your wounds, and yet you know that all you can do is to keep fighting, then it is good to be reminded of Paul and 2 Corinthians 4. Ultimately the battle is the Lord's, the Church is the Lord's, and the victory has been won for all eternity.

Although we will be put to the test, and there are likely to be times when we are tried and found wanting, the deeper truth is that we do not fight in our own strength or in our own resources. We are carried in the strength and the grace God gives. This was the experience of Paul. So he says in 2 Corinthians 12:10, 'Whenever I am weak, then I am strong', and in verse 9 he writes, 'He said to me, "My grace is sufficient for you, for my power is made perfect in weakness."' What Paul is describing here is the reality of life 'in Christ Jesus', where Jesus Christ is Lord and we are the servants of others for Jesus' sake. It means being carried by God when we no longer have the resources in ourselves to continue the work.

Paul says, 'We urge you also not to accept the grace of God in vain' (2 Corinthians 6:1). This was the verse sent to me before my ordination in a short letter from a priest in the Diocese of Natal, who had been my university chaplain and who had played an important role in nurturing my own vocation to the priesthood. He wrote, 'This may seem an odd thing to say at the time of your ordination, but this verse was given to me by an older priest when I was ordained, and it is something that I have come back to again and again.' To be rooted in Jesus is to become more and more dependent on the grace of God in Christ.

This is the work of the Holy Spirit in us. When we talk about being 'led by the Holy Spirit', we are really talking about being 'transformed' by the indwelling presence of God's Spirit (see Romans 12:1–2 and 2 Corinthians 3:17–18).

In this inward journey of personal transformation I become, over a lifetime, the person God created me to be, Christ-like but in my own unique way. To put it slightly differently, through God's Spirit we discover who we really are, as God's beloved sons and daughters. We increasingly learn (and this can be slow, hard work), to live out this awareness, not just in our words and deeds but by our entire way of life.

The ongoing transformation is critical because as part of this process God's Spirit is slowly opening our spiritual ears and eyes to see and hear more clearly what God is saying and doing. It is essential if we are going to be able to follow him as he calls us to do, and is what being led by the Spirit is all about.

My friend and fellow priest from the Diocese of Natal Andrew Judge writes, 'I have come to understand spiritual growth not in terms of moral improvement but rather of seeing and hearing more clearly (with Jesus' eyes?) what is going on in my life and around me in the world. As we start to see things in an increasingly godly way, our attitudes and behaviour will change. This is transformative change, from the inside out.'[29]

The love of God is poured into our hearts

Paul writes, 'And not only that, but we also boast in our sufferings, knowing that suffering produces endurance, and endurance produces character, and character produces hope, and hope does not disappoint us, because God's love has been poured into our hearts through the Holy Spirit that has been given to us' (Romans 5:3–5). Can you imagine the love of God being poured out, like water from a vast fountain or river, into your own heart? This is such an important image, because unless and until God's love starts to become a personal reality and not just head knowledge, we lack the motivation and the courage to embark on this journey intentionally. We need God's love to be poured into our hearts if we are to cooperate with what God wants to do in us, which will involve dethroning the ego, the centrality of 'me' and 'self'.

As we become more and more deeply held by the unfathomable and infinite vastness of God's love, we are able to enter into the profound work of transformation. We are the beloved of God, in Christ Jesus our Saviour. This is the foundation, the fulcrum, the *sine qua non*, of Christian life and ministry—and so it was for Paul. In his great prayer in Ephesians 3:16–19 he says, 'I pray that, according to the riches of his glory, he may grant that you may be strengthened in your inner being with power through his Spirit, and that Christ may dwell in your hearts through faith, as you are being rooted and grounded in love. I pray that you may have the power to comprehend, with all the saints, what is the breadth and length and height and depth, and to know the love of Christ that surpasses knowledge, so that you may be filled with all the fullness of God.'

Paul is stretching the limits of his vocabulary and the powers of his imagination as he tries to say, 'May you somehow be given power to comprehend the love of Christ, which actually, in fact, surpasses the limits of human knowledge and understanding.' This love surpasses even breadth and length and height and depth; it is like the sky and the sea and the vast horizon, reaching even beyond the sky and the sea, the depths and the height and then more (how can we take it in?), so that somehow, by the grace of Christ and the power of the Holy Spirit, we may be filled with all the fullness of God.

Chapter 8

Jesus calls us to rest

O God, from whom all holy desires, all good counsels, and all just works do proceed: Give unto thy servants that peace which the world cannot give; that both our hearts may be set to obey thy commandments, and also that by thee we being defended from the fear of our enemies may pass our time in rest and quietness; through the merits of Jesus Christ our Saviour. Amen

THE SECOND COLLECT AT EVENING PRAYER, THE BOOK OF COMMON PRAYER

I WAS DRIVING on a busy road with two lanes of traffic, constantly contending with big trucks and speeding drivers, making my way to another meeting. I used to enjoy the adrenalin that driving gave me. Now it has become an effort. The world seems to have speeded up, year by year, and we don't notice it happening until we say, 'This is not how life should be.' Where is the space, the peace, the balance between excitement and rest and boredom? It is a very long time since I last even experienced boredom. Once I could listen to music only by going to a concert or by playing a record on my record player or by listening to the radio. Now I have 860 songs on my iPod and another 300 CDs in a cupboard. We have movies and TV shows on demand, and all major sports events can be watched live on television. No longer do I have to rely on listening to the commentary or the sports news on the radio.

The adrenalin-fuelled life can be a lot of fun, but it can also become exhausting. Where in this fast-moving, driven world do I find rest? How can I speak of resting in Christ when I know that each day brings a new set of challenges, pressures and demands?

The rest and restoration that our hearts long for are promised to us by Jesus. Jesus says, 'Come to me, all you that are weary and are carrying heavy burdens, and I will give you rest. Take my yoke upon you, and learn from me; for I am gentle and humble in heart, and you will find rest for your souls' (Matthew 11:28–29). If ever there was a promise of Jesus for 21st-century Western people, this is it. We sometimes feel that we have everything except the time to enjoy what we have. We are the tired generation. Jesus invites us to come to him and to learn from him. What is it that he asks us to learn? Perhaps it is the self-emptying, the letting go of the old drivenness and striving that characterises the false self, and the releasing of our hearts into new and deeper trust in him.

Jesus says, 'Learn from me; for I am gentle and humble in heart.' As our hearts become more and more like the heart of Jesus, which is gentle and humble, we will find rest for our souls. Learning from Christ, and being rooted in Christ, is the way to the rest and the restoration he offers.

When we know in our hearts that we are truly safe and secure in the love of God for us, we will find a quality of rest that the world cannot give us. Paul tells us that 'neither death, nor life, nor angels, nor rulers, nor things present, nor things to come, nor powers, nor height, nor depth, nor anything else in all creation, will be able to separate us from the love of God in Christ Jesus our Lord' (Romans 8:38–39). This is the truth that enables us to live as a people of hope in the midst of struggle and testing.

Refreshment for body and spirit

Rest is, above all, a gift from God. It is a gift that in our culture we seem to find increasingly difficult to accept. I heard an inspector of schools speaking on the radio recently about some of the problems in the education system. 'We need to do more,' he said. This sums up the prevailing work culture in our society. It's about always needing to do more. It's not about finding time 'to be'.

In Isaiah 30:15 we read, 'In returning and rest you shall be saved; in quietness and in trust shall be your strength. But you refused and said, "No! We will flee upon horses"—therefore you shall flee!' Our deepest need is to return to the Lord who gives rest and peace to our hearts. Rest comes first of all from God. It is in our hearts that we will find true rest. In quietness and trust we will come to know that the love of God is the answer to our deepest longings.

Rest is also practical. God made us to work and to be creative, as indeed God himself works and is the creator. But he also made us for rest, as he himself rested on the seventh day (Genesis 2:2). Sabbath rest is written into the very beginning of the created order. God rested, and he created us for work and for rest. Work and rest are both equally God's purpose for us. Pope Francis has lamented the end of the traditional Christian day of rest, saying on a visit to southern Italy, 'Maybe it's time to ask ourselves if working on Sundays is true freedom.'[30]

An important question for those in ministry to ask regularly is, 'Am I getting enough rest?' In recent years I have sometimes wondered if I even know how to rest any more. To rest is to cease from work; in a sense, to rest is to cease from activity. When an athlete rests, he or she stops running. How hard it is these days for many of us actually to stop running?

Rest leads to restoration. I remember being told when I was young that sabbath rest did not mean doing nothing; it meant doing anything that brought relaxation and restoration. This is true, of course. But something has gone wrong when I try to fit a mini-break in Prague into three days of a long weekend before starting another busy and demanding week at work.

The rest that we most deeply need will come from our returning to the Lord and finding our peace in him. This is not just a 'spiritual' issue. My body, mind, emotions and my soul are all part of what makes me the person I am. Rest is needed in every part of my being. Sleep is a critical part of this rest. We still do not fully understand the mysteries of the restoration that takes place during the hours of sleep. Other dimensions of rest will be found through taking proper care of ourselves. We must pay attention to the need for good nutrition, regular exercise, healthy daily habits and the wise use of alcohol, caffeine and medication.

As we grow in the practice of contemplative prayer, we are likely to become more aware of those aspects of our behaviour that are hindering the peace and rest which God is bringing to our hearts. We become more tuned into subtle patterns of addictive behaviour, such as overeating or watching too much television or the compulsive need to buy and acquire more stuff. Electronic media can become a particularly addictive part of our daily lives and as contemplatives we will be uncomfortable if such activity starts to intrude too much into our consciousness.

We may also become more aware of the ways we experience stress and anxiety in our bodies and in our reactions and responses in daily life. As this happens, it is good to ask God for the grace and help we need to change our ways of living, and trust that by his Spirit he will lead us to a new and more healthy and life-giving place. In all of this, the key word is compassion. God looks on us with unfailing compassion and love. He cares for us, says 1 Peter 5:7. It is not surprising that God's will for us, and his peace, is made known to us as we learn to care better for ourselves.

We have a right to rest

It is true that we have a right to rest. We are not called by God to work without ceasing. Many of those in full-time ministry find themselves working 60, 70 or maybe 80 hours a week. Some of us have more stamina than others. Some are called to roles of significant responsibility, which can be very costly and personally demanding. For each one of us, rest is part of our vocation. If we forget this, we may pay the price with burnout, exhaustion and family break-up. We need a godly discernment as to how God is calling us to spend our time and to use our energy, which are both finite.

Ignatian spirituality offers a helpful process of discernment, first developed by Ignatius of Loyola, and widely used in Christian spirituality. One of the key components in Ignatius's teaching is the criterion of selection which uses the Latin word for 'more', *magis*. We look at the choices we face in life, and we first examine ourselves to see if we are seeking our own interest and advantage rather than the good of others. When we have done this, we may find ourselves faced with different possible courses of positive action. We then may ask, 'Which of these alternatives will lead to more of the peace, love and justice which are at the heart of the kingdom of God? Which will bring about more compassion, more joy, more faithfulness, more fruit of the Holy Spirit?'

In our present culture the word 'more' can be problematic. God is not always asking for more, in the sense of more hard work, more people to visit, more time in prayer, and so on. God's desire for us is that we should seek first his kingdom and his righteousness (Matthew 6:33). The longing of the true self is for more of God, more of his love, more of his peace, more of compassion. In his book *The Art of Discernment*, Stefan Kiechle SJ writes, 'God never makes excessive demands on anybody. That is why human beings should engage themselves according to their individual strengths and abilities. We need to consistently check our actions in order to avoid any tendency to do too much or too little. Doing too much is currently more fashionable.'[31]

Blessed and broken

In Luke 24 there is an account of how Jesus, after his death in Jerusalem, met two disciples on the road to Emmaus and walked with them. They were on a journey, and after the events in Jerusalem they were tired, confused and disillusioned. Jesus listened to them. He spoke to their hearts. He stayed to eat with them, took bread, blessed and broke it, and gave it to them. And everything changed. 'They said to each other, "Were not our hearts burning within us while he was talking to us on the road, while he was opening the scriptures to us?"' (Luke 24:32).

The two disciples on the road to Emmaus found that as a result of meeting Jesus on their journey, their lives were transformed and their despondency and weariness vanished. As I have reflected on this account, I can begin to see how Jesus reveals himself to me and restores me through the blessing and breaking of my life. I am like the bread which Jesus takes, blesses, breaks and gives to his people and to his world.

I am blessed by God in so many ways. My home, my family, my work, my health, the beauty around me and the love and kindness and friendship I experience daily—these are all extraordinary gifts and blessings from the hand of God. These are the signs to me each day of God's unending love. It is good to pause every day and to reflect with gratitude on the amazing goodness of the Lord to me and my family.

But with the blessing also comes the breaking. I cannot be given unless I am also being broken. That old 'me first' self is being broken so that the new self that is rooted in Christ can be formed in me. Spiritual formation is the process, each day, of being made more and more like Jesus for the sake of others. This does not happen without a cost. The ways of the false self are deeply rooted in us, and we do not easily let go of what drives us, and especially of the need and desire for control and approval. To learn to live in complete dependence upon God is a long journey for us all, but it is the way to finding the rest for which our hearts are longing.

As I reflect on my own experience in Christian ministry, it seems that, over many years, God has been at work in me by his Spirit, teaching me to depend more and more upon him in every aspect of my life. This is still a work in progress. I have to learn each day anew to let go, and to let God be God.

Isaiah 30:15 tells us that it is in quietness and in trust that we shall find our strength, and in returning and rest we shall be saved. We have to stop our desperate rushing around, our relentless busyness, and return to the Lord. Before him we have nothing to prove, for he loves us infinitely and unconditionally as we are. In the Lord alone we will find the rest we desire.

Part Five

Letting go

Chapter 9

Let go and let God

O Lord, we beseech thee to keep thy Church and household continually in thy true religion; that they who do lean only upon the hope of thy heavenly grace may evermore be defended by thy mighty power; through Jesus Christ our Lord. Amen

THE COLLECT: THE FIFTH SUNDAY AFTER THE EPIPHANY, THE BOOK OF COMMON PRAYER

CONTEMPLATIVE MINISTRY and spiritual formation go hand in hand. As we seek to deepen our relationship with God, we are formed daily into becoming more like Jesus in our character and our behaviour. I have discovered, sometimes the hard way, that this involves learning to let go and let God be God.

I remember many years ago, when I was studying at Natal University in South Africa, a student friend said to me, 'There is a great truth in this, Ian: let go and let God.' This somehow stuck in my mind and in recent years I have come back to it in a new way. I have never been very good at letting go. I can see now that being in control has been important to me in much of my life—and letting go of that need is a long and complex process. But we do have to learn to 'let go and let God', and the place where much of this work is done is the place of prayer.

Paul knew about letting go. In Philippians 2:5–7 he writes, 'Let the same mind be in you that was in Christ Jesus, who, though he was in the form of God, did not regard equality with God as something to be exploited, but emptied himself, taking the form of a slave, and being born in human likeness.' Letting go is a kind of self-emptying. Paul says that we should have the same mind or attitude as Jesus, who let go of all that was his by right. He emptied himself and took the form of a slave, of someone with no rights at all. Jesus was not forced to do this; he did this freely, so that he might be totally and unconditionally available to do the will of his Father. Letting go of all of this enabled Jesus to humble himself and become obedient to the point of death—even death on a cross (v. 8). To let go means to surrender, so that God's perfect will may be accomplished in us, whatever that may mean.

A passage which spells out what letting go meant for Paul himself is found in Philippians 3:7–13.

Yet whatever gains I had, these I have come to regard as loss because of Christ. More than that, I regard everything as loss because of the surpassing value of knowing Christ Jesus my Lord. For his sake I have suffered the loss of all things, and I regard them as rubbish, in order that I may gain Christ and be found in him, not having a righteousness of my own that comes from the law, but one that comes through faith in Christ, the righteousness from God based on faith.

What does it mean to gain Christ and to be found in him? One of the many aspects is that we surrender all that we cling to as being of real value in this life, and that we cling instead to Christ, as the One who is all in all to us. The problem lies in the clinging, not the things we value. This letting go is not easy for anyone but is the path we are called to walk if we are followers of Jesus. In life's journey there are many times when we will be broken, if we have not learnt how to bend like a tree in the wind. Someone who always knows best, who is always right and does not brook correction from others, is a person who is heading for a fall. Life is constantly trying to teach us about letting go and about surrender, and what we refuse to surrender is often taken away. If we don't learn willingly, we may well have to learn the hard way.

I was listening to a contemporary worship CD in my car recently. The worship leader was singing that everything he was belonged to the Lord and that he was laying it all down at God's feet. This is the letting go that we have to come back to again and again, the process that is always incomplete because there is always more to surrender. We can sing 'I surrender all', and at that moment we may truly mean it with all our hearts, but the truth is that, although we may at that point in our worship have surrendered all, it won't be long before we have taken some of it back!

I think that God is trying to teach us all about letting go, in many small ways and sometimes in very big ways. My daughter Grace was married in July 2013. It was a wonderful day in so many respects, but I also found it daunting to be the father of the bride, with all that this means. There is a letting go indeed. Every time a child moves to a new school year, or we reach another birthday, or see the end of one more summer, there is another letting go. It seems important in our own spirituality to acknowledge the centrality of letting go.

In June 2013 I was surprised and somewhat shocked when I read the 'God's Politics' blog by Sojourners founder and noted Christian leader and writer, Jim Wallis. This was not the usual kind of 'God's Politics' topic at all. Instead, Jim Wallis described, in a very personal account, his experience and his reactions to receiving out of the blue a diagnosis of prostate cancer. The blog was called, 'Losing control and learning to trust: my unexpected diagnosis'. He wrote:

I spoke with a few close friends before going in for my cancer surgery, a day full of anxiety for someone who had never faced a major health issue before. My old and dear friend, Wes Granberg-Michaelson, contrasted our need for control with the 'Prayer of Abandonment' by Charles De Foucauld. So I went back to that classic prayer, and found it the right one to take into surgery for someone who had been totally preoccupied with the absolute craziness of an 18-city book and media tour and was now facing a very personal health crisis.

I abandon myself into your hands;
do with me what you will.
Whatever you may do, I thank you:
I am ready for all, I accept all.

Let only your will be done in me,
And in all your creatures—
I wish no more than this, O Lord.

Into your hands I commend my soul:
I offer it to you with all the love of
my heart,
for I love you, Lord, and so need to give myself,

to surrender myself into your hands without reserve,
and with boundless confidence,
for you are my Father.

It was a perfect prayer for surgery and recovery, and I hope one I remember before my next book tour! A week after surgery, my

*wonderful colleague at the publisher Brazos/Baker, B.J. Heyboer,
wrote me what a member of her discernment committee for the
Episcopal priesthood had said to her: 'Control is an illusion, an
illusion that we all pursue. But the sooner you see it as the illusion
it is, the better off you—and your ministry—will be.'* [32]

Prayer as letting go

In prayer we can come daily to practise this choosing
of surrender, of letting go. Here in the place of prayer we
accustom our hearts to the deeper work of the Holy Spirit
in leading us to the surrender of self-will, which is central to
following Jesus.

Prayer is essentially relationship with God, and so it makes
sense that in our daily place of intimacy with God, we practise
the letting go of our own thoughts and ideas and agendas. In
the contemplative way of praying we do and think as little
as possible, in order that we may simply be in the presence
of God 'just as I am'. The more we do this, the more we will
be ready to trust God when the tough challenges of life come
our way, as they surely will. In contemplative prayer we let
God be God, and we wait upon him, knowing that all things
are in his hands.

To learn this way of being with God has meant a significant
shift in my own way of praying. Much of my early Christian
formation as a student in South Africa was in the evangelical
world. We were taught as young Christians to aim to have
a 'quiet time' at the beginning of every day. I would find a
quiet place, probably in my bedroom, and would have with
me my Bible, a notebook, some daily Bible reading notes
and an intercession list. This time of prayer—starting each
day with God—was regarded as very important. It was

almost as though missing my quiet time meant that the day wasn't going to be quite what it should be. This discipline and training laid the foundation for much of my subsequent spiritual journey.

When I moved to Salisbury and we set up 'The Contemplative Minister' days, I began to read books by writers such as Henri Nouwen and Thomas Merton with new insight. Although I had taken regular Quiet Days in order to spend time alone with God for many years, I had never practiced contemplative prayer as a daily discipline. Through Sue Langdon and Darrell Weyman, the leaders with whom I began working in Salisbury, I learnt that contemplative prayer is not an optional extra in this way of life. It is at the very heart of it.

The model of prayer which Sue and Darrell recommend is Centering Prayer as taught by Thomas Keating and Cynthia Bourgeault. Essentially this is the prayer of surrender. They encourage those attending the course to aim for 20 minutes of Centering Prayer, either once or twice a day. This is of course in addition to the other ways in which we pray, such as the daily office, Bible study or *lectio divina*, and intercessory prayer.

In his book *Open Mind, Open Heart*, which has sold over half a million copies in English alone, Thomas Keating describes the practice of Centering Prayer and Welcoming Prayer. This is based on three key aspects of the emotional programmes for happiness, which we all develop as we grow up. These key aspects are the desire for power and control, the desire for safety and security, and the desire for esteem and affection. They tie in closely with the three temptations which Jesus faced in the wilderness, the temptations for security and physical provision (bread), for power (the kingdoms of the world and their splendour) and for esteem ('If you are the Son of God...') (see Matthew 4:1–11). Through the practice of Centering Prayer and the Welcoming Prayer we learn to recognise these deep desires and emotions when they grab hold of us in one way or another, to welcome them, and then, probably quite slowly and gently, to let go. Thomas Keating writes, 'The Welcoming Prayer is a way of "letting go" into the present moment in the ordinary routines of daily life. The Welcoming Prayer is used when your needs for security, affection, and control are frustrated or gratified and cause emotional reactions.'[33]

It is important not to short-circuit these deep emotional needs, but to focus on them and allow them to sink in and simply experience the sensation. We may say something like, 'I let go of my anger,' or 'I give my anger to God.' Then we can in due course say, 'I let go of my desire for power and control. I let go of my desire for safety and security. I let go of my desire for esteem and affection.' Keating says, 'Letting go means passing through the experience, not around it, not running away from it, or stuffing it back into the unconscious.'[34] We remain in the bodily sensation, and gently and quietly say the word 'welcome'. At the heart of this process for me is the letting go of my desire to control or change the situation or circumstances which I face, and placing my trust entirely in God for whatever outcome may lie ahead. Again, this is saying in a telling and profound way, 'I surrender.' We are saying, 'I am in entirely in your hands, O Lord. Put me to living, put me to dying. I will trust in you regardless. I know that nothing in all creation can separate me from the love of God in Christ Jesus my Lord.'

Letting go means coming to the point, as Jim Wallis says, of losing control and learning to trust. The truth is that we don't really learn to trust until we learn that we are not in control. Sooner or later we have to place ourselves utterly and unconditionally in God's hands. We have to let God be God. We spend our whole lives learning more and more to trust and depend upon the grace of God which is in Christ Jesus. If we can do this day by day, in our daily praying—letting go in love, and letting God be God—this will profoundly change us over time and transform us into those for whom Christ truly is Lord.

Chapter 10

Letting go in love

I USED TO BE a marathon runner. I loved to run. Running, for me, was being alive. For me, there were few greater joys than being physically fit, and being able to get up early on a summer morning, put on my running shoes, and set out across the hills for a 20-mile run. Then I would arrive back home at about 7 am, have a shower and a good breakfast, and begin the day's work.

Unfortunately, I cannot do this any more. Long-distance running has a tendency to find the body's weaknesses eventually, and sooner or later you get injured. Some of these injuries become long-term problems, and you may end up having to give up running altogether. My weakness is my feet. I have rigid high-arched feet, and over the years I have had a number of foot problems and a few operations along the way as well. Then I developed something called plantar fasciitis, an inflammation of the main supporting fascia on the sole of the foot. My wife and I went to Italy for a short holiday, and when we returned, my feet were in a bad way. I thought they would soon get better but I then discovered that plantar fasciitis is one of the most stubborn and painful fascia injuries, and it takes a long, long time to heal. For nearly a year I found that I could do only a minimum amount of walking and standing. The problem is that if you are standing on a damaged fascia, you are simply making the injury worse. This has been a difficult and challenging experience, especially for someone who loves to be active, to go walking and move around freely. I have discovered, first-hand, a little bit of what it is like to be a disabled person.

In the past my approach to problems like this has been based on making them go away as quickly as possible. When I go to see the doctor, I want him or her to fix my problem, which is why surgery is an attractive option. You have the operation, and then you get on with life again. So I went to see a highly respected foot and ankle surgeon. He said to me, 'Plantar fasciitis is horrible. It will get better eventually. If I see you in six months' time, your feet will be 50 per cent better than they are now.' He didn't even want to talk about surgery. That was six months ago at the time of writing, and I think he was right. I am now a lot more mobile than I was, but I still regularly struggle with the pain on the soles of my feet.

I was talking about this to a friend, an Anglican priest, who is disabled and suffers with both pain and disability. She said to me, 'Ian, it's OK to sit when others are standing. There are a lot of people who live with disabilities, and when they see you sitting, they will know you understand what it's like for them.' My disability has been comparatively minor but it has given me new insight into the reality that so many disabled people experience. It's very hard when you can no longer simply go where you want to go or stand in line for a coffee or enjoy a 'normal' holiday.

All true spirituality is about what we do with our weakness. Paul was able to say, 'So, I will boast all the more gladly of my weaknesses, so that the power of Christ may dwell in me... Whenever I am weak, then I am strong' (2 Corinthians 12:9–10). We cannot learn to depend upon the grace and power of God unless we have learnt our own weakness. Being strong and self-sufficient feels good to the false self, but the true self does not need to prove anything to other people. The true self is content for me to be who I am before God, as his beloved child, with all my weaknesses and with no pretending. I can let go knowing that his grace is sufficient for me, and all will be well, because I am eternally held secure in the love of God.

In a mysterious way I suspect that God even uses disabilities like my injured feet to lead me deeper into trusting him. It's hard to sit when others are standing, but in reality this is largely because of my preoccupation with appearance, with what others are thinking. That's the false self again. I love to be strong and in control, walking and running like everybody else. In reality not everybody is strong. We all carry our wounds and weaknesses, and we learn how to hide them, sometimes even from ourselves. God sees and knows us as we really are, and his Spirit is at work in us to enable us to live publicly the truth of who we are before him.

Letting go is important for us all because, sooner or later, some things that are important and dear to us will be taken away, sometimes permanently. What do we do with this reality? It can be very hard and challenging to the human spirit, but there is a way through. Part of this is learning to accept and trust the grace and faithfulness of God, even in our deepest need. Part of this also is being thankful for the mercies that surround us, the kindness and love of family and friends, and even strangers. We learn to depend more upon God and to depend more on one another. It is even possible to thank God for the disability and the deprivation, because it brings us closer to important realities: what really matters, and all that endures and that forms human character in grace, love and wisdom.

Surrender/no surrender

When we are faced with the problem of suffering, we are dealing with mystery. David Jenkins, former Bishop of Durham, wrote in his 1966 Bampton Lectures, 'I am clear that Jesus Christ enables us humanly and hopefully to face evil. I do not yet see that he enables us to explain evil.'[35]

Surrender and letting go is not some simple answer to the reality of pain and suffering. There is a time to surrender but there is also a time to resist, to fight against evil and pain, distress and disease. John Dalrymple was a Scottish Roman Catholic priest and the author of many bestselling books on spirituality. He wrote movingly of his own struggle with suffering and weakness, following two heart attacks, prior to his sudden death in 1985. Dalrymple says, 'A common misunderstanding about the Christian attitude to suffering is to say that we should simply accept it uncomplainingly.' He points out that throughout his life Jesus resisted suffering and sickness wherever he went. 'Jesus was killed on the cross because he fought against suffering and sickness, not because he accepted it. In fact he was persecuted and put to death because of his non-acceptance of suffering and sickness.'

Jesus knew that his opposition to the suffering and oppression around him was leading him into confrontation with those in authority. Dalrymple says, 'On many occasions he avoided confrontation with his enemies, taking refuge in neutral territory. It was only when he could no longer avoid confrontation without compromising his principles that he saw that his death was the Father's will. Then he accepted it, embraced it, offered it up for the redemption of mankind.'[36]

For Dalrymple, following Jesus means that we are called to fight against suffering with all our strength, and also to accept suffering and surrender ourselves to what we cannot change, and what therefore seems in some sense to be God's purpose for us. He says, 'There is clearly a paradox here, but unless we stress both the fight against and the acceptance of pain, we do not understand the full meaning of suffering as Christ suffered.'

My own experience with my foot injury has echoed what Dalrymple is saying. I have tried to do everything that I can to bring about healing in my feet. I have seen doctors and physiotherapists. I've had sports massage and acquired expensive orthotic supports. I've put ice packs on my feet every day and done all the stretches recommended for this problem. A good friend, a doctor, said to me some time ago, 'Ian, this will take 18 months; maybe two years.' So the other side of dealing with this has been learning to accept it. It will probably get better eventually, but it will take a long time.

In the meantime, in the midst of the frustration, there is much for me to learn. I am reminded of what John Wimber said as he reflected on the story of Jacob, who wrestled with God and bore the mark of this struggle (Genesis 32:24–32), that we should never trust a Christian leader who does not walk with a limp. Our weaknesses are the raw material that God uses to make us holy, if we will only work with him in the process of transformation. Of course, it is costly and difficult for us, but through learning to let go in love, and let God into our lives, we will become more and more those in whom God's loving purposes can be accomplished.

I have therefore aimed to use my own disability to deepen my practice of contemplative prayer and of letting go. I am in God's hands; he will do with me according to his will. I can trust him for this; I can rest in him. I am learning to live one day at a time, in dependence on God. I know, more than ever, that it is important to live within my limits, and to work out what this means for me if I am to live a more holy and whole life.

Many of us have an ideal planted in our minds of the man or woman that we would like to be. This may be the person who is always in control, cool and confident. Confidence is everything, says the popular culture. If I have the right clothes, the right haircut, the right body, I will be able to have whatever I want because it's my appearance that counts. If I look cool and sound cool, then I am cool. I recall, when I was younger, seeing Steve McQueen or Paul Newman in a film, and walking out thinking, 'Maybe, somehow, I could be like that.' Of course, this is an illusion, but in a world where our culture constantly feeds us images of success and power and whatever is 'cool' we have to be very careful as to what is ruling our hearts. If I am not being myself, I am likely to pretend to be something that I was never made to be. The reality of who I am is that I am not always strong, confident and in control. The sooner I give up this illusion of control the better off I will be.

Two years ago I had the privilege of spending some time in Scotland with James Finley, who served as a novice for a number of years under Thomas Merton. Finley came to know Merton well, and he has written extensively about Merton, and about the contemplative life. James Finley said that, in finding our true selves, the last frontier of ego-based consciousness is to yield, to surrender, to let go. It is so difficult for us and in Christian spirituality this is often associated with 'the dark night of the soul', a period of spiritual crisis (after a poem by the Spanish mystic St John of the Cross). Letting go of the need to be in control, and letting go of the fear of failing, is essential to the transformation of the inner life.

James Finley says, 'Shortcomings, both real and imagined, when deeply seen and accepted, are an important part of the transformative process of learning to let go. If we do not let go of the need to be perfect, our need to be perfect will get in our way. Likewise, if we do not let go of our fear of failing, our fear of failing will get in the way. But as we learn to let go of the need to be perfect and the fear of failure, the intimate, earthy stuff of being a vulnerable, loving human being begins to shine through. In an ongoing process of learning to let go we bear witness to the great truth that the master limps.'[37]

So what is a contemplative? A contemplative person is someone who has learnt to let go, in particular of the desire to be in control and the fear of failing, and who has learnt to listen, to be attentive and to yield to the will of God whatever that may be. Contemplation is an intimacy with God, a wordless resting in God beyond all our thoughts and words and strivings. To be a contemplative people and a contemplative church we must pause from our activity and busyness, to reground our hearts in God, without whom we are nothing.

That is the heart, the essence, of contemplative ministry.

Part Six

Contemplative Living

Chapter 11

The rules and exercises of contemplative living

Almighty God, who hast given thine only Son to be unto us both a sacrifice for sin, and also an example of godly life: Give us grace that we may always most thankfully receive that his inestimable benefit, and also daily endeavour ourselves to follow the blessed steps of his most holy life; through the same Jesus Christ our Lord. Amen

THE COLLECT: THE SECOND SUNDAY AFTER EASTER,
THE BOOK OF COMMON PRAYER

JEREMY TAYLOR (1613–67) was an Anglican priest who grew up in Cambridge, the son of a barber. He was taken prisoner with other Royalists during the time of Oliver Cromwell and the English Civil War. Eventually he became Bishop of Down and Connor in Ireland. His book *The Rule and Exercises of Holy Living* was published in 1650, and was soon recognised as one of the classics of English devotional writing. It was followed in 1651 by *The Rule and Exercises of Holy Dying*.

Holy Living by Jeremy Taylor reflects the Puritan ethos of the time, with a strong emphasis on sin and the remedies that are required if we are to avoid the causes of sinning in order to be holy. This does not make for comfortable reading for those whose view of life has been formed by 21st-century culture. However, there is much in Taylor's writing to make us take notice, if we are serious about the call to holy living. What does holy living mean? For Taylor it is a call to put God first in every aspect of our lives, and to make the service and love of God our ultimate goal in life. If we truly love God, we will want to spend as much time with him as we can. We will also want every part of our lives to be pleasing to him and will therefore shun all activities and attractions that may draw us away from God or cause us to sin. As Jeremy Taylor wrote, '... although it cannot be injoined, that the greatest part of our time be spent in the direct actions of devotion and religion, yet it will become, not only a duty, but also a great providence, to lay aside for the services of God and the businesses of the Spirit as much as we can: because God rewards our minutes with long and eternal happiness.'[38]

In Christian understanding holy living is the same as contemplative living. It is practising our faith by living each day intentionally in the presence of God. The Catholic theologian Keith Egan describes the Christian religious meaning of contemplation as 'an intensification of a transforming awareness of divine presence. Contemplation transforms one's spiritual resources and effects a deeper practice of virtue'.[39]

This vision of a life lived in the presence of God, and for the glory of God, is at the heart of Jeremy Taylor's writing. Every part of daily life, every duty and every natural function, can be drawn to God and given to him. James Taylor declared, 'Only it becomes us to remember and to adore God's goodness, that God hath not only permitted us to serve the necessities of our nature, but hath made them to become parts of our duty; that if we by directing these actions to the glory of God intend them as instruments to continue our persons in his service, he by adopting them into religion may turn our nature into grace, and accept our natural actions as actions of religion. God is pleased to esteem it as a part of his service, if we eat or drink, so it be done temperately, and as may best preserve our health, that our health may enable our services towards him: and there is no one minute of our lives (after we are come to the use of reason) but we are or may be doing the work of God, even then when we most of all serve ourselves.'[40]

Any contemporary rule of life or set of exercises of contemplative living is likely to be framed as a set of values, or 'contemplative stances', rather than as a group of rules or laws. Their purpose will be to enable us to offer the whole of our daily life to the glory of God. A Christian rule of life for 21st-century people is not a matter of simple rules and regulations. It is about acquiring wisdom and putting it into practice, through anchoring the way we live our lives in certain key principles or values. A rule of life has been described as 'the Spirit-empowered rhythms and relationships that create, redeem, sustain and transform the life God invites you to humbly fulfill for Christ's glory'.[41] This is not legalism but something that enables us to draw close to Christ by committing ourselves to a particular pattern of daily life, which will assist in the development of holy living. A rule of life is a flexible and adaptable invitation, a way of growing into God's grace day by day.

Many people are familiar with the importance of a rule of life within the monastic tradition, particularly the great rule of St Benedict. This has been widely written about in recent years as being relevant for Christians seeking to live out their faith in today's world. In particular Esther de Waal's book *Seeking God* speaks about the importance of listening, of stability, of balance, and of finding God in the ordinary things of everyday life. Esther de Waal writes, 'St Benedict seeks God in the most simple and ordinary experience of daily living. He is not looking for any special thoughts, ideas or feelings to feed a religious life. His starting point is simply what one present-day monk calls "the stark reality of the humdrum".'[42]

A rule of life, in the Benedictine sense, is for everyone— not just for 'special' religious or ordained people. Every one of us has a vocation to be holy, which means, very simply, to live close to God.

Another more contemporary rule is *The Rule of Taizé* from the Taizé community in France, which welcomes thousands of young people from all over the world, who go as pilgrims to Taizé every year. The Rule of Taizé speaks of 'The Acts of Community' and 'The Spiritual Disciplines'. Here we see two key concepts in understanding what a rule of life is. This is about community and about how we live in community with one another.

The Acts of Community are Prayer, The Meal, The Council and Order. A few simple rules are given concerning the conduct of prayer, mealtimes, the community council and general order and punctuality. 'The Spiritual Disciplines' are described as follows: 'Throughout your day let work and rest be quickened by the Word of God; maintain interior silence in all things, in order to dwell in Christ; become filled with the spirit of the Beatitudes; joy; simplicity; mercy.'[43]

It is important that Christians are people who live out what they profess to believe. A significant problem for the church in much of the Western world is that it is not seen as a credible model of discipleship. I heard of a US American television personality who was interviewing a group of American Christian leaders. He said, 'The problem with you guys is that you Christians don't practise your religion.' On the other hand, Muslims and Buddhists and Hindus are seen to be those who 'practise their religion'. They are regarded as having a credible spirituality which is based on the way of life practised by the adherents of those faiths.

A rule of life can be a helpful way of addressing this issue, perhaps particularly for younger Christians. It is a practical way of getting to grips with how we live the Christian life. You can call it discipleship, or spiritual formation, or simply 'practising our religion'.

If we follow the insights of St Benedict, we will see that this is something that can work for anyone. It doesn't matter who you are, whether you're a student at university or a commuter going into the city on the train, or a retired person spending a lot of time at home on your own. Joan Chittister, in her book *Living the Rule of St Benedict Today*, writes, 'Benedictine prayer is not designed to take people out of the world to find God. Benedictine prayer is designed to enable people to realise that God is in the world around them.'[44]

A rule of life is a way of offering ourselves to God, in all the ordinary circumstances of daily life, and also in the extraordinary circumstances in which we sometimes find ourselves. In the autumn of 2011 I was given three months' study leave to do some thinking and reading around the subject of contemplative living. For me, contemplative living means finding a way of life that is centred in God. I wanted to explore what this actually looks like, especially for those of us who live busy and active lives. There are principles or values that lie at the heart of this way of living, of what it means to have a rule of life which draws us closer to Christ. This is another way of thinking about spiritual formation. How are we formed by the Spirit of God to become more like Jesus, in the service of others?

An awareness of the classical spiritual disciplines can help us to gain a clearer picture of this way of living. Richard Foster's excellent book *Celebration of Discipline* has been helpful to many Christians in renewing an understanding of spiritual disciplines and the principles upon which they are founded. Richard Foster describes twelve classical disciplines of the spiritual life. He divides these into three categories: the inward disciplines (meditation, prayer, fasting and study), the outward disciplines (simplicity, solitude, submission and service) and the corporate disciplines (confession, worship, guidance and celebration). Foster writes, 'We must not be led to believe that the Disciplines are for spiritual giants and hence beyond our reach, or for contemplatives who devote all their time to prayer and meditation. Far from it. God intends the Disciplines of the spiritual life to be for ordinary human beings: people who have jobs, who care for children, who must wash dishes and mow lawns. In fact, the Disciplines are best exercised in the midst of our normal daily activities. If they are to have any transforming effect, the effect must be found in the ordinary junctures of human life: in our relationships with our husband or wife, our brothers and sisters, our friends and neighbours.'[45] He emphasises that this must not become a return to 'another set of soul-killing laws'.[46]

This is a journey towards holiness and towards wholeness in Christ. It is the work of the Holy Spirit in us, in which we give ourselves day by day to God, through practical commitments, through service and through sacrifice. In this process we ourselves are changed and so become more and more deeply rooted in Christ. This is truly the work of spiritual formation.

Chapter 12

Spiritual formation

O God, who, through the preaching of the blessed Apostle Saint Paul, hast caused the light of the Gospel to shine throughout the world; Grant, we beseech thee, that we, having his wonderful conversion in remembrance, may show forth our thankfulness unto thee for the same, by following the holy doctrine which he taught; through Jesus Christ our Lord. Amen

THE COLLECT: CONVERSION OF ST PAUL, THE BOOK OF COMMON PRAYER

ON 25 JANUARY each year the Anglican Church, together with many other Churches, celebrates the conversion of St Paul. Saul of Tarsus met the risen Jesus on the road to Damascus, and his life was completely changed. Instead of persecuting the early Christians because of his zeal for his Jewish faith, he led the proclamation of the Christian Gospel to the Gentile world.

Since then there have been many remarkable conversions in the history of Church. Stephen Lungu was a young gang leader in what is now Zimbabwe, who went to a Gospel tent meeting with home-made bombs, with the intention of throwing the bombs into the tent and shooting anyone who tried to escape. However, as Stephen heard the Gospel message, his heart melted and he was converted to Christ. He himself became an evangelist and eventually became the international team leader of African Enterprise, a leading African evangelistic organisation.

Conversion is central to Christian faith. Being converted to Christ means turning away from sin and turning towards God. The result is a transformation, a personal interior change that leads directly to a new way of living in the power of the Holy Spirit. At the beginning of Mark's Gospel we read that 'Jesus came to Galilee, proclaiming the good news of God, and saying, "The time is fulfilled, and the kingdom of God has come near; repent, and believe in the good news"' (Mark 1:14–15). Conversion comes about through repentance, literally a change of mind, and through believing in and following Jesus Christ. However, it is important not to think of conversion as a one-off experience. I remember a bishop in South Africa saying, 'Baptism is not the event of a moment, but the principle of a lifetime.' This is also true of conversion. We live our conversion daily, as we live our baptism.

In 1981 Jim Wallis wrote an influential book entitled *The Call to Conversion*, in which he challenged evangelical Christians to face the full implications of the biblical understanding of conversion. Wallis writes:

If we believe the Bible, every part of our lives belongs to the God who created us and intends to redeem us. No part of us stands apart from God's boundless love; no aspect of our lives remains untouched by the conversion that is God's call and God's gift to us. Biblically, conversion means to surrender ourselves to God in every sphere of human existence: the personal and social, the spiritual and economic, the psychological and political.

Conversion is our fundamental decision in regard to God. It marks nothing less than the ending of the old and the emergence of the new.[47]

Conversion does not simply apply to the personal and the individual spheres of life. It applies to every aspect of human life, including the economic, the political and the social. The claims of Christ are not simply about private religious behaviour. His claims cover the whole of life and every part of human experience.

Conversion is inextricably tied to the lifelong work of spiritual formation. As we are changed by the work of the Holy Spirit within us, we become, day by day, more like Jesus. In this journey we do not always move forward, but instead sometimes seem to vacillate, or even to go backwards, before moving to a new and deeper integration of Christ into our way of living.

Henri Nouwen has described this journey as a series of spiritual movements, from 'this' to 'that', from what hinders and holds back our life in Christ, to what brings freedom and true peace and joy. Nouwen writes, 'Spiritual formation, I have come to believe, is not about steps or stages on the way to perfection. It's about the *movements* from the mind to the heart through prayer in its many forms that re-unite us with God, each other, and our truest selves.'[48]

In his book *Spiritual Formation*, Henri Nouwen sets out seven movements in spiritual development.[49] These reflect the thinking that is present in a number of Nouwen's other books, such as *Reaching Out* and *In the Name of Jesus*. The seven movements are:

Early Movements
1. From Opaqueness to Transparency
2. From Illusion to Prayer

Midlife Movements
3. From Sorrow to Joy

4. From Resentment to Gratitude
5. From Fear to Love

Mature Movements

6. From Exclusion to Inclusion
7. From Denying to Befriending Death

Nouwen's thinking is helpful in clarifying our understanding of the purpose of spiritual disciplines. As already mentioned, these are not intended to be rules and regulations, but practices and principles to enable us to grow into maturity in Christ. The series of movements in the spiritual formation of those who are led by the Holy Spirit unfold over the course of life's journey, leading us towards transparency and openness, contemplative prayer, joy and gratitude. As we enter more and more deeply into this journey, our hearts are led from fear to love and compassion, and from excluding and labelling others to an inclusive generosity and hospitality. The final movement in the spiritual life is from denying to befriending our own death, 'in radical trust in the one who loved us before our birth and will be with us after death'.[50]

In my own journey, I have found that there are eight spiritual disciplines of contemplative living which are vital for me if I am to live my conversion daily and respond to the work of the Holy Spirit in me. Some of these overlap with the aids to contemplative prayer that I explored in Chapter 5.

Silence and Solitude

The practice of daily silent prayer enables us to become rooted in Jesus and his self-emptying love. There are many ways of finding the opportunity to be still in God's presence. We will seldom experience pure silence. Even in a quiet place in the countryside there is the sound of the wind in the trees, and the birds and creatures around us. Most of us will not easily be able to escape the sound and presence of other human beings. But we can find a place to be still, and to experience a sense of the silence that draws us closer to God. A friend of mine said to me recently that she is helped by attending the early morning Book of Common Prayer service of Holy Communion in her local church. She described this as being contemplative worship. I also find this increasingly valuable.

We are surrounded by noise, and our heads and hearts often seem to be spinning with the endless stuff that comes at us from every direction. We need practices and places to provide for us a withdrawal from noise and rush and busyness. We must seek silence and solitude from time to time if we are to sustain any depth of relationship with God who reigns in infinite silence and majesty.

Simplicity

Living simply is a way of addressing the surplus of everything, the burdens and distractions that crowd into our thoughts and lives. We live in an age of excess. Many of us have a sense of unease about the surfeit of goods, of food and drink and all manner of good things which are continually offered to us to buy and consume. In 2008 the World Bank estimated that over 2.5 billion people worldwide live on less than $2 a day, with nearly three-quarters of the population of sub-Saharan Africa falling into that category.[51] We need to do some hard thinking here. Simplicity is a moral as well as a spiritual imperative for all who follow the teaching of Jesus. If we don't take specific steps to live simply and to give generously, we are missing some central parts of the words of Jesus. Jesus said, 'No one can serve two masters; for a slave will either hate the one and love the other, or be devoted to the one and despise the other. You cannot serve God and wealth' (Matthew 6:24).

As followers of Jesus, we are to love our neighbour as ourselves, and hold a particular care for the hungry, the stranger, the sick and those in prison (Matthew 25:44–45). The implications of this are not difficult to work out, but are sometimes difficult to practise, because our hearts are still held by our material possessions. Essentially what we should aim for is as follows. Live simply. Resist extravagance. Give away the things that you have but do not need. Ask yourself before you buy something, 'Do I really need this? What is God saying to me about this?' Give generously. Consider the biblical standard of giving away one tenth of your income (tithing). Then give some more, to the poor, the hungry and the refugees. It is a good principle of faith to give more than we can humanly afford, because this leads us to a greater dependence upon God for the provision of our needs.

Detachment

Detachment is sometimes understood as a kind of indifference, even apathy—the opposite of engagement and commitment. In reality, detachment is very different from indifference. Detachment is about letting go and putting all our trust in God. We remain passionate about God, about justice, about love and compassion and holiness. We do not take ourselves too seriously, because we know that everything is in God's hands.

Through detachment we embrace weakness and anonymity. We no longer need to be in control and to be noticed. Daily life provides us with many opportunities to learn detachment.

When I am stuck in a traffic jam on a motorway, thinking about the meeting or the appointment I am missing, I can choose to be angry and frustrated. Alternatively, I can recognise that the situation is beyond my control, and that all I can do is wait until the traffic starts moving, and in the meantime listen to music or ponder and reflect upon what is happening around me. When my flight is delayed or I become ill at an inconvenient time (illness is always inconvenient in my experience!) then the same choices lie before me.

Paul knew the meaning of detachment. 'I have learned to be content with whatever I have. I know what it is to have little, and I know what it is to have plenty. In any and all circumstances I have learned the secret of being well-fed and of going hungry, of having plenty and of being in need. I can do all things through him who strengthens me' (Philippians 4:11–13). Much of this is about knowing in whom our strength lies. The real test, of course, comes when I am weak or hungry, or ill, or in pain. Through detachment I discover who I really am when I let go of all the stuff I think I need to be strong and in control of my life. I acknowledge my weakness, my utter dependence upon God. I gain a sense of proportion about the things that happen to me which seem to mess up my plans for a short while. I don't need possessions or achievements or titles to bolster my status and authority. The compulsions and the illusions that drive so much of our society lose their power and allure. Detachment, like simplicity, is freedom—the freedom to which Christ calls each one of his beloved disciples.

Attentiveness

In pastoral ministry we often find ourselves exercising a three-fold listening: listening to God, listening to the other person and, at the same time, listening to ourselves, to our own reactions and concerns. This skill often takes years of training and experience to develop. It is not easy to be a good listener. We don't often experience being listened to by someone who gives us their full attention and interest for a sustained period.

The mark of a contemplative attitude is an increasing attentiveness to others, to our own hearts and to God. This is an essential quality of spiritual direction and is the key to much pastoral ministry. There is no shortcut to being a good listener. To be truly attentive to the present moment and to the person or people alongside us, we must leave behind our thoughts about the past and the future. We let go of all distractions, even as they come into our view, and we simply come back to the still centre, to the present moment. This is not easy, and the quality of our attentiveness will vary enormously, depending on what is happening in our lives at the time.

We can train ourselves in becoming more attentive. The primary way to do so is through the daily practice of contemplative prayer. There are many other ways, however. I am a keen birdwatcher, and I have found this to be a good way to learn about attentiveness. When you are watching for birds, you have to be still, sometimes for quite a long time, and wait. Only then do the birds come out, often silently, and suddenly... there is a redwing or a sparrowhawk. The great thing about birdwatching is that you never know what is going to appear. Seeing an unusual bird always gives me a thrill, a sense of surprise and joy. Common birds are also worth watching—the robin hopping up and down on the grass, the pigeon lazily resting, perhaps even falling asleep, on the roof. A friend of mine had to spend long hours sitting quietly at home through physical weakness. He watched a pigeon fall asleep on a rooftop and slowly lose its footing as it drifted off. Suddenly it fell, woke up, flapped its wings and flew away. My friend said that this was something he would never have seen had he not been sitting there, gazing from his veranda for hours.

Gratitude

Gratitude flows out of attentiveness. As we open our eyes to see, and our ears to hear, we become more and more aware of the goodness and beauty all around us. As we learn to live simply and to move away from always wanting more, we find joy and contentment in the abundance before us. The beauty of the sky and clouds, the laughter of friends and family, the treasures that lie within books and music: all of these and so much more, are rich gifts from the hand of God.

It seems to be a strange paradox that the more we own, the harder it becomes to enjoy to the full the abundance we have. In a sense, we are made for simplicity, not for excess. A grateful heart knows that these gifts are not ours by right; they are gifts and not possessions, and so we are grateful. I recently visited the cottage Clouds Hill in Dorset, which was the home of T.E. Lawrence, otherwise known as Lawrence of Arabia. After the end of World War I, Lawrence preferred to live quietly and simply in obscurity. He chose solitude and lived in a quiet woodland, alone with his books and music. As I sat in Clouds Hill, I recognised within myself the longing that Lawrence must have known when he returned from the desert, to be free of the pressures of Western culture. Simplicity opens the door to clarity of thinking, to gratitude and wisdom. Thanksgiving is a constant theme in the Psalms. 'Give thanks to the Lord, for he is good' (Psalm 136:1); 'I will give you thanks, O Lord, with my whole heart' (Psalm 138:1). A good measure of our heart's intimacy with God is the degree to which thanksgiving springs up in us through each day we live. The opposite of gratitude is complaining. Do we complain a lot? There is no great joy in listening to someone complaining. Gratitude, however, is always a blessing.

We can use all our senses to know God's presence and love with us through each day. Poetry and art, music, the beauty of nature: joy is close at hand as we travel through each day of our lives. Let us give thanks to the Lord, for he is good and his mercy endures forever.

Community

Contemplative living is not something that we can do alone. We will be called to times of solitude, but even those who live alone are normally part of a community of some form. We live not only 'unto ourselves'; we live for others, and through others we become our true selves. To be human is to be part of a family and a community. In African society this is understood very well. The Zulu word *ubuntu* means 'one-anotherness' in the sense that I am only a person in and through my relationships with other people. There is no direct equivalent for *ubuntu* in the English language, yet it is something that is greatly needed as the tide of individualism grows ever stronger in Western culture.

Many people in our society are looking for community of some kind or other, and this applies particularly to young adults, the generation for whom society seems to offer very little that is secure or stable. For many of this generation, the fruit of the culture of individualism and 'doing my own thing' has left them with some sense of family, although often fractured, and their friends, but with almost nothing else to rely on, to trust. The question many are asking is, 'Who is going to be there for me when I need a friend?' Community is the future of the Church, as it has been the key to Christian life and the growth of the church from the very earliest times. In the UK Soul Survivor youth events, which draw thousands upon thousands of young people each year, there seem to be three key values: worship and spending a lot of time in God's presence; friendship and building relationships; and a passion for the lost and the broken. This is an example of what Christian community means for the emerging generation. In valuing community we build especially on our relationships with those we meet each day: our families, our friends, our colleagues and our neighbours. These are the people that God gives to each of us, through whom we experience the reality of love. We find Christ in one another.

It is important to recognise that ministry and community belong together. A model of ministry that is not rooted in local community is missing something very important. We cannot do this alone; we need one another. We need our friends, our neighbours and our colleagues. We need to be able to share our lives, the joys and the struggles of ministry. Community is an essential spiritual discipline for all in public ministry.

Servanthood

If we are being led by the heart of Jesus, we will be led to the poor, the hungry, the lost, the broken-hearted, those in prison. The Gospels make this absolutely clear. 'The Spirit of the Lord is upon me,' declared Jesus in Luke 4:18, 'because he has anointed me to bring good news to the poor.' In Matthew 25:40 he says, 'Truly I tell you, just as you did it to one of the least of these who are members of my family, you did it to me.'

In my years of ministry in South Africa I saw many churches becoming increasingly aware of the call of Jesus to go to the poor, to cross the boundaries of the rich and the safe areas, and to build relationships with those living in townships and informal settlements. The Church of the Ascension in Hilton, near Pietermaritzburg, where I was rector for eleven years, developed a substantial ministry over a long period of time with the community of Sweetwaters, where there is extreme poverty. Many times I visited people who lived in small mud huts, with only newspaper to cover the floor, and a few broken pieces of furniture or wooden boxes and planks. Again and again, we were welcomed with great warmth, and many times I knew that in some mysterious way I had been with Jesus in the presence of the poor. There is something about taking on the role of a servant, especially the servant of the poor, that brings us close to the heart of Jesus. What is required is the willingness to go as he went, empty-handed and with only our caring and our desire to say, 'Here I am; I come as your friend.' Then we may also be able to say, 'Is there anything we can do to help?' It is perhaps more important to say first, 'What is the gift I can receive from you today?'

There are countless opportunities before us each day to practise servanthood. Every time someone needs a listening ear or a helping hand, a visit or perhaps a meal, is a God-given opportunity to offer the care of Jesus. His heart is a servant heart, gentle and compassionate. The heart of Jesus reaches out to the weak, the helpless and the forgotten. As our hearts are attuned to his heart, we will know more and more of his care for those around us.

In a sense, the contemplative Church is the Church of the poor. It is the Church of each of us who know their need of God, because we have come to know our own weakness and woundedness. The heart of God reaches out to the poor and weak, and so the contemplative Church is the Church that welcomes and cares for all who are poor, broken and helpless.

Self-discipline

Our generation is perhaps not well equipped to practice self-discipline. My grandparents believed that self-discipline was the key to good character and was in itself virtuous. Our age is a consumerist, hedonistic age, and many believe that we have a right to gratify our appetites wherever we can. Often it is good to say 'no' to something, not because it is in itself evil, but simply because I have grasped what is truly important in life, and I desire to 'apply myself wholly to this one thing, and draw all my cares and studies this way' (see The Book of Common Prayer, 'The Ordination of Priests').

To grow in the practice of holy living, it will be necessary for us to make wise choices in order to take good care of ourselves. We pay proper attention to caring for our bodies, through healthy eating and drinking, through exercise and rest. We care also for our minds, through reading, study and reflection.

We live in an age where 'work hard, play hard' is often the prevailing ethos, but this may not be helpful for many of us. If we are conscientious by nature or driven or ambitious, we may well consistently push ourselves and those around us far harder than is good for us. I have tried over the years to learn to be gentle with myself and with those I love, remembering that Jesus himself is gentle and humble in heart, and that he leads me to wholeness and to find rest for my soul.

Part Seven

Becoming a contemplative church

Chapter 13

Learning servant leadership

IN 1979 Henri Nouwen wrote a book called *The Wounded Healer*. The book became a spiritual classic, as much as anything because of Nouwen's insight that our capacity to bring healing to those who are broken is directly related to our acceptance of our own woundedness. Nouwen wrote:

The minister is called to recognise the sufferings of his time in his own heart and make that recognition the starting point of his service. Whether he tries to enter into a dislocated world, relate to a convulsive generation, or speak to a dying man, his service will not be perceived as authentic unless it comes from a heart wounded by the suffering about which he speaks.'[52]

In finding our true selves, we have to experience the dying of the false self. This is not an easy or painless process. It is a matter of death and resurrection. Jesus talked about the grain of wheat that must fall to the ground and die before it is to bear much fruit in due time (see John 12:24).

At the heart of the call to follow Jesus is the cross. As Jesus emptied himself and took the form of a servant and became obedient unto death (see Philippians 2:5–8), so we who follow him will be called to the same self-emptying obedience. We cannot separate the call to serve Christ in ministry from a daily dying to self and to all that hinders the life of the Holy Spirit in us.

My early years in ordained parish ministry were marked by a whole-hearted commitment to serving God, and a lot of hard work. There was the joy of seeing God at work, and also a lot of pain, particularly in the 14 years that I was in parish ministry in South Africa. In 1994 I was appointed rector of All Saints', Milton, a church on the north side of Cambridge in England. Milton is a village close to the Cambridge Science Park, where there had recently been a large-scale housing development. The years in Cambridge were good in many respects. We worked hard, the church grew, and there was much fruit. But I was increasingly aware that I was coming to a crossroads in my understanding of God's call to me. I had written three books. I had been widely involved in church leadership in Cambridge and across the region. I had applied for a number of appointments in large evangelical churches in different parts of the country. For some of these I was called to be interviewed, but none was actually offered to me.

I felt a deepening sense of frustration. I felt that I had done the work that God had brought me to do in Milton. It was time to move on, time for someone else with different gifts to come to lead this church in the next stage of its life and growth. What was I to do next? I had been to see the bishop, and he was very affirming of the work that I had done, but he had no particular advice as to how I was to find my next appointment. He encouraged me to keep my eyes open for suitable jobs that might come up, and to see what happened.

My interest in spirituality had begun in South Africa when, during one particularly tough time in ministry, I had discovered the value of having a spiritual director. This concern with a deepening of my inner life and my relationship with God had grown during my time in Cambridge. I had been able to complete the Spiritual Exercises of St Ignatius in daily life, sometimes known as the Nineteenth Annotation. This took around ten months, and involved a weekly meeting with an experienced spiritual director in Cambridge. The Spiritual Exercises of Ignatius focus on using the imagination in prayer to enter more and more deeply into the life, passion, death and resurrection of Jesus. Looking back, I can see that this was a significant part of the shift in my sense of my vocation and ministry taking place during these years.

The second half of life

At the time when I did the Ignatian Exercises, I was 47 years old. I have since discovered that this is often a pivotal point in the movement from the first half of life to the second. The first half of life is, for many people, characterised by the need to accomplish goals, to do all the things that seem to have been set before us as we set out upon adult life. Our energy and our time is spent on establishing our careers, possibly getting married and having children, setting up a home and working to become successful in what we have chosen to do. In the second half of life the focus shifts. Achievement and success become less central to our view of our lives. We tend to be more concerned with finding a measure of contentment and peace with ourselves, with who we are and what we have become. What matters in the second half of life is not so much what others think of us as what we think and how we feel about ourselves.

I also found myself asking some uncomfortable but important questions about my understanding of ministry.

Why did I keep looking for bigger and more important jobs? Is there really such a thing as an important or significant church? Why did I aspire to be the leader of such a church?

I had learnt from ordained colleagues in the Methodist and Roman Catholic Churches when I was in South Africa that in some churches once you are ordained, you agree to go wherever the church sends you. I started to ponder whether I was going about my search for a new job in the wrong way. Was this really how God wanted his ministers to discover where they were most needed in the service of his kingdom? Applying for attractive-sounding jobs that I had seen advertised in church magazines became an increasingly tedious task. Surely there was a better way than learning how to present myself and my strengths and gifts to maximum advantage in a CV and job application, and then going through a competitive interview, only to discover that this was apparently not where God was calling me after all. Something about the whole process just felt wrong for me at that time.

I decided to try a different and altogether more risky approach. I went to see the bishop and said to him, 'I need to move on from my present parish. Where do you want me to go? I am willing to go wherever I am needed.' The bishop looked at me and thought about this for a short while. 'Will you go to Yaxley?' he said.

I replied that I would certainly look at going to Yaxley. St Peter's, Yaxley, is on the south side of Peterborough, and about 30 miles from Cambridge. It may be in Cambridgeshire but it is a different world from the university city of Cambridge. A large parish of over 10,000 people on the edge of the Fens, St Peter's, Yaxley, had a long and troubled history. The congregation was dwindling. My predecessor had died in post. His predecessor had left under difficult circumstances, and his predecessor had also died in post. So no priest had left St Peter's happily and well for over 30 years. There was a very considerable resistance to change, and little understanding or experience of mission or discipleship. When I phoned the local area dean, he said to me, 'Ian, it's a sleeping giant. It's just waiting for someone to come and wake it up.'

So I said to the bishop that I would be willing to go to Yaxley. I had no real idea of what lay ahead of me, but all my experience of ministry led me to believe that God is committed to his church and that I could depend upon the Holy Spirit to do a new thing in Yaxley. This would be a new challenge, a kind of ministry different from anything I had previously experienced. I would be radically dependent on God. That seemed to me to be a right and healthy place to be.

It proved to be far tougher than I ever anticipated. A new way of being church was not what some of the congregation were wanting. I was not 'a proper vicar', I was told, and I should go back to Cambridge. They didn't want my sort of priest in Yaxley. I faced a scale of conflict, bullying and resistance to change that I had never previously experienced in any church. I soon understood some of the reasons why my predecessors had found the parish difficult.

But, remarkably, things began to change. New people were drawn in to the life of the church, and our work among children and young people started to grow and flourish. Soon the Sunday worship had a very different, more contemporary feel, and there was a real sense of life and growth. In 2007 we were able to reorder the church interior and install a new heating system, which transformed this beautiful ancient building. For this we raised nearly £150,000, an astonishing sum for St Peter's. We gave one tenth of this to help build a new church in Maseru, Lesotho, in one of the poorest countries in Africa. In June 2007 I stood at the top of one of the mountain passes in Lesotho with a group from St Peter's, Yaxley, who had travelled all that way to visit the congregation of St Andrew's, Maseru East, as mission partners. I knew then, beyond all doubt, that God had in an amazing way vindicated my obedience in going to Yaxley.

The future of Christian leadership

I learnt a lot from this time. I learnt in a whole new way to give up the search for a higher position and to accept the call to serve. Something in me, which was at its heart a form of pride, of 'Ian-centredness', needed to be broken, and there was no easy way for this to happen. I had to become willing to serve Christ on his terms, not mine. I needed to learn to go where I was most needed, rather than to accept only the opportunities that I would prefer.

During this time I read a book by Henri Nouwen called *In the Name of Jesus* several times. In this book, Nouwen writes about his vision of the future of Christian leadership. He speaks of a movement from relevance to prayer, from popularity to ministry, from leading to being led. He writes, 'The leader of the future will be the one who dares to claim his irrelevance in the contemporary world as a divine vocation that allows him or her to enter into a deep solidarity with the anguish underlying all the glitter of success and to bring the light of Jesus there.'[53]

Going to Yaxley was my response to the understanding that I had to stop chasing success and relevance and positions of leadership. I had to be willing to take up in a new way the call to servant ministry, with all that this might entail, including unpopularity, irrelevance and pain. In my time at Yaxley I experienced all these in ways that have marked me deeply. At the same time I saw God at work, and I know now that there were things about the life of following Jesus that I simply would not have learnt without my time in this difficult and testing, but ultimately glorious, place.

We are not likely to become contemplative ministers without experiencing the pruning work of the Lord. We have to face some hard questions. Would we be willing to go, if called, to the people and places where we are most needed? There are many uncongenial parishes, places where there is much deprivation and brokenness and need. Who will go to these places? Are we prepared to be 'buried' in Christ's service, to go somewhere where no one will notice what we are doing (or perhaps not doing)? Much of the work of Jesus is done among the poor, in hidden and lonely places, where most, if not all, of the work, the faithful and sacrificial service, is known to God alone. Will this be enough for us?

Christ calls each of his followers to servant ministry. All those in ordained ministry in the Anglican Church, and in many other Churches, are ordained first of all as deacons. Deacons are called to service, to be ambassadors of Christ in the world, attending to the needs of others and especially the poor, the marginalised, the weak and the lonely. Are we prepared to walk this costly path? Servant ministry and contemplative ministry are two sides of the same coin. Both are about being formed more deeply into the self-emptying nature of Christ. Both take us down the road of learning to let go and let God be God. This is the work of the whole of life's journey; it is not easy and it takes a long, long time. Henri Nouwen described it as the future of Christian leadership, this way that is radically dependent on Jesus and which proclaims him to be Lord, with us as servants for Jesus' sake (see 2 Corinthians 4:5). It leads to a contemplative way of being church that is centred on listening and serving, on building community and on a way of living which is both counter-cultural and missional. This emerging Church, this contemplative Church is showing the way to the future of Christian ministry and mission in the 21st century.

Chapter 14

Reconnect:
a contemplative church

PAUL BRADBURY is a Pioneer Minister and the leader of the Poole Missional Communities. An Anglican priest, he was appointed by the Diocese of Salisbury in 2008 to reach people in Poole, on the Dorset coast, who would not otherwise be reached by traditional forms of Church. Paul lives and works with his family in the central area of Poole and his appointment was in response to a rapid growth in population in Poole, mainly through high-density housing development, and to the need for new models of mission and ministry to connect with those moving into this area.

Since then a number of linked communities have grown out of the original missional community, which was called Reconnect. There is now a café on the High Street in Poole, as well as 'Space for Life', a community of some 25 women based around textiles, arts and crafts, which meets once a week. There is also 'Work Space', which aims to connect with people in the workplace, meeting in the borough offices. The ministry continues to unfold and develop with different expressions of community emerging in different contexts. Poole Missional Communities is one of a number of Fresh Expressions of Church that have a contemplative centre to its life and mission.

I spoke to Paul Bradbury and asked him how the ministry had begun.

Paul: After I was appointed, there was a very deep commitment to listening, because we had all sorts of ideas and things we wanted to do. But we didn't know Poole, we didn't know anybody, so my approach was simply to listen, to understand what kind of a place Poole was, its history, what sort of people lived here; also, where the church in Poole was in terms of mission. What was it doing? What was it not doing?

Also, we were deeply committed to getting a sense of what God wanted us to do. We had this idea of *missio dei*, of God already at work in the community, in mission. How could we listen to what the Spirit was already doing? Where was he inviting us to join in with what he was already doing? So we spent six months praying and listening, talking to people, prayer walking, praying with others, building relationships. And then a second six months was spent beginning to develop this into a mission, and communicating that vision to those we were beginning to get to know.

Ian: During that first six months what did you actually do in terms of starting a church?

Paul: Not a lot, really. We were just laying the foundations. We were not even sure that we wanted to start a church at all at that stage. Our approach was very much to find ways of serving and listening and loving people, and building community, and then exploring discipleship out of that. In due course we started a missional community, a church. This was because I came to the conclusion that the most powerful thing that we could do to reach out to unchurched people was to model Christian community to them. One of the most powerful vehicles of mission is the church itself; not what the church does but what the church is. The church is modelling the kingdom as individuals, but also, most powerfully perhaps, as community to those around us. So people around begin to say, 'What is it about this group? Why are they living in a counter-cultural way?' People begin to belong to that community because they are interested in it, and inspired by it, and then they begin to explore the faith that lives at the heart of it. So we did plant a church, not to do something whizzy and different on a Sunday that might attract people, but in order to live out the Gospel.

Ian: A rule of life has been central to the development of the Missional Communities. Tell me more about that.

Paul: The first thing we did as a community when we started Reconnect, with nine adults, was that we met weekly in the evenings and we developed a rule of life. We didn't start by asking, 'How are we going to worship?' We started by asking, 'How are we going to live?' We didn't start by saying, 'What is our statement of doctrine?' We said, 'We are Anglican and orthodox and Christian. Let's park that for a while. The most important thing we want is to ask is "How do we want to live together?"' We went back to Acts, to the Gospels, the Sermon on the Mount and thrashed that through, over six to nine months. Then we developed a series of statements that try to express, as succinctly as we could, how we wanted to be and to live together as a community.

This is not a residential community. It's a dispersed community in the location of central Poole. We are trying to ask ourselves what is important to us as we read the Gospels and as we read Acts. If we are really taking this seriously, what does this mean?

Ian: What are the values that are at the centre of your rule of life?

Paul: That Jesus is Lord. The first statement is that Jesus is Lord, that Jesus is not just somebody we believe in, but we believe the things that Jesus believed. So if Jesus is asking us to live simple lives and to live generous lives and hospitable lives, then that is what we believe too.

We start with the statement that we are making Jesus Lord in our lives, and we break that down to various aspects that we read from the Gospels and Acts, about generosity and hospitality, about healing and prayer and worship.

It includes the importance of the Bible, and the importance of being an open community, and of inviting people to follow Jesus. We also talk about justice—justice for other human beings, and also justice for creation—so there is an element of caring for the earth and the environment.

Ian: This seems to have been particularly attractive to people who are not part of traditional forms of church.

Paul: Yes, increasingly so. I'm not sure to what extent it is the rule of life as such or the way that it's lived out. One of the people who has joined Reconnect recently said that what attracted her was that we are a non-materialistic group of people. We are not always talking about money, our latest purchase. On the contrary, we talk about simplicity, about not needing this and not needing that.

Ian: To what extent have you geared the ministry here to be aimed at unchurched people?

Paul: I think people are fundamentally not so much asking, 'What should I believe? What can I believe? What is the truth?' Those questions have not completely gone away. But I think that in our post-modern culture, people are asking, 'How can I live? What foundation for living is going to make a difference, to help me to live well?' I think people are beginning to recognise the deficiencies of consumerism and individualism and of a lack of community. They want community. They want a simple life. They want a less busy life, and they are not quite sure how to get there. The eternal questions of what I should believe in order to get to heaven, didn't seem to me to be as 'up front' as 'How can I live well?'

Ian: Tell me how you have used contemplative prayer as part of establishing the work of Poole Missional Communities.

Paul: As part of our listening, I wanted to listen more deeply to people who are not going to church. So I developed a questionnaire, which I took to mother and toddler groups, to homeless shelters, and other places where I could meet people who were outside the church. I spoke to 30 people and asked them about their spirituality because I wanted to know what their experience of God was. I didn't want to ask them about church, about beliefs, but about God. The vast majority of people said 'yes' to the question, 'Do you have a sense of God?'. When I asked, 'How do you express that?' about 50 per cent said, 'I pray or I meditate.' There seems to be a vast number of people who don't go to church who are actively practising prayer or meditation as a way of connecting with God. So I thought that surely must be a way to connect with them.

There is a latent spirituality out there, and if we can point that in the direction of its origins, surely we can connect with people and direct them towards Christ.

With Poole town centre, I felt that because it is a place where people come to work, we had to explore how we could connect with the workplace. I thought that the work place is getting increasingly frenetic and busy and pressured. If we could offer half an hour of quiet contemplative prayer, we hoped this would connect with some of those people who are exploring spirituality, but it would also connect with well-being, and with posing the question, 'Do you really want to be working flat out all the time? What about attending to other aspects of who you are? What about attending to your soul?' We have done that in Barclays' House, which is one of the major employers, and also in the RNLI, and we continue to offer that in the borough offices in the Civic Centre in Poole.

Ian: You have also had a focus on spiritual direction, primarily for those who are spiritual seekers rather than those who are already Christians.

Paul: This is something we would love to grow more, but this is emerging at the moment. My wife is a trained spiritual director, and she feels a call to use this with people who are not currently going to church, and is at present directing two or three people. I think this is a powerful way of engaging with people. Many are nervous about the Church as an institution, or about organised religion in any form, but want to go on a spiritual journey. So offering them a guide for that journey can be something to which they are very receptive.

Ian: I was very struck by your sense that your worship is not simply about holding services on a Sunday but that it flows out of your rule of life and your life as a community. Can you explain that a bit more?

Paul: I see our Sunday gatherings as the community coming together. We are involved in worship and in ministering through the whole of the week wherever we are. Worship is all of life. So we gather all of this together on a Sunday. We gather the stories of the week, and we ask, 'Where has God been?' and 'Where has God not been?' We resource one another to go out into the world again. I try to ensure that our worship is deeply connected with people's lives, with people's work and their situations and sometimes with what is going on in the world.

We don't have a programme for our worship. Whereas a lot of churches will follow a sermon series or the lectionary, we have very informal, participative worship. I encourage those leading worship—and we have many people who lead worship, not just myself—to lead out of where they are, so that immediately it is connected with what is going on in their lives, rather than thinking, 'I've got to lead worship from Luke, chapter 5.' It means that it is a bit random in terms of themes! We do observe the major Christian festivals, so that we are rooted in the Christian story through the calendar. The rule of life gives us a structure throughout the year, in looking at each phrase, and perhaps we will explore one aspect of this for a term. Other than that, we are connecting with the life of the community.

Ian: In thinking about becoming a contemplative church, it seems to me that the future of the Church lies in a model which is primarily a servant model, which values deepening our lived experience of knowing Christ, above structures and outward appearance and show.

What is your thought about the future of the Church, and about what it means in our culture to become a contemplative church?

Paul: We have deliberately moved away from a model that is consumerist by nature. What I mean by that is putting on a service on a Sunday, and it might be charismatic evangelical, or it may be high Anglo-Catholic, but it's essentially reaching out to people who enjoy that kind of worship. We didn't want to attract people from other churches to the latest quirky alternative. We wanted to reach unchurched people. Worship is not the shop window to church. Our lives, lived out in community, are the shop window. The relationships that we build with people are what we hope will bring people to belonging and to faith. The nature of our worship will flow out of that.

Our worship is changing. We can't assume that the way we worshipped when we first started, as nine people who had been used to going to church, will be the same now, when 25 per cent of our community have no experience, or only a very distant one, of going to church.

So we are ditching that (sometimes conscious, sometimes unconscious) sense of 'putting on a show', which can take a huge amount of time and resources. We encourage our community to ask, 'How can I use my gifts? How can I use what I already do? How can I use my hobbies? My workplace? What communities am I already involved in?' This is about doing church where life is already happening. We encourage people to be missional disciples. We have sometimes disconnected those two terms, as though all of us are disciples, but only some of us are missionaries. It's as though being missional is a particular talent or gift of certain people, rather than part and parcel of what it means to be a disciple.

Ian: Do you see being missional and being contemplative as not opposites but integral to one another?

Paul: Definitely. We understand being contemplative in the sense of deeply listening to the context and constantly asking the questions, 'Where is God in this context? Where is God in my workplace? How can I join in with what God is doing?', and also listening to ourselves.

'Space for Life' is the classic example of asking people to listen to what they could offer in mission. Two of our original nine people said, 'We are both felt-makers, which is a bit unusual. Why don't we offer felt-making as a way of growing community?' So they did. They started offering felt-making workshops, which were very popular. That turned into a regular group which diversified into textile arts and knitting and sewing. This has now emerged as something that is rapidly becoming church for people.

Ian: Is there anything else you would like to say about Poole Missional Communities?

Paul: For me personally, and also for us as church, the letting go, the downward mobility, has been a constant challenge, because we live in a wider church culture that still glorifies the large churches and the leaders of those larger churches. It often feels as if the leadership of the institution is looking over your shoulder and asking, 'How many people come to your church?' The contemplative approach to ministry is about constantly letting go and saying, 'It's not about us as an organisation, as a sizeable church. This is about doing what God is calling us to do, and trusting that this will bring fruitfulness.'

What we are doing is long-term stuff. It's putting down those roots of a rule of life and encouraging a counter-cultural approach to ministry, which is hard.

It's been tough for me, because all of us can be attracted to the idea of being the leader of a large church, and all that goes with it. It's tough to feel constantly that you are laying this down in order to grow a missional movement that has a much greater chance of sustainability and 'reproducibility' in the long run.

Chapter 15

Transformation

O God, of unchangeable power and eternal light, look favourably on thy whole Church, that wonderful and sacred mystery; and, by the tranquil operation of thy perpetual providence, carry out the work of our salvation; and let the whole world feel and see that things which were cast down are being built up, and things which had grown old are being made new, and that all things are returning to perfection through him from whom they took their origin, Jesus Christ thy Son our Lord.

GELASIAN SACRAMENTARY, FOR THE CHURCH

IN MARCH 2014 I was invited to attend a service of thanksgiving for the life and work of Nelson Mandela at Westminster Abbey. It was an extraordinary event, attended by many leaders and famous people. The sermon was preached by Archbishop Desmond Tutu. This was a grand occasion, and for many there was a sense of the importance and privilege of being present as we formally gave thanks to God for the life of Nelson Mandela, in the spectacular setting of Westminster Abbey.

For myself, however, and I suspect for a number of other South Africans present, this occasion evoked mixed emotions. The example and the life of Nelson Mandela has been remarkable. At his death, the world seemed to stop for a moment to say, 'This man has something to teach us all. He has shown us the way to a better, more human, more just and more compassionate world. We need to listen to him.' He was, without doubt, one of the great figures of the 20th century.

South Africa has experienced a wonderful transformation in the last 20 years, since the first democratic elections in 1994. I was there during the time leading up to the transition to majority rule; I voted in those first elections and will never forget that day. I am clear in my own mind that South Africa experienced a miracle. To see one human life miraculously changed through conversion, as happened to St Paul, is amazing. To see a nation miraculously transformed is beyond what most of us can take in. And yet, it happened. Very few of us who grew up in the 1960s and 1970s in South Africa dreamed that we would ever see the non-racial South Africa that exists today. South Africa still has many problems; inequality and poverty have not gone away, and many people live their lives in deprivation and great hardship. In many ways, South Africa is a microcosm of the global village. The rich and the poor, the strong and the weak, are all neighbours on this small planet, but in the Western world we can often get on with our lives without noticing our poorer neighbours, who grow much of the food we eat and make many of the clothes we wear. In South Africa all are there together: the world in one country.

I give thanks to God for the life of Nelson Mandela. I give thanks for the transformation of my country, South Africa. It is indeed beyond what I ever expected, perhaps even hoped for. To see groups of young black and white women and men standing and chatting and laughing as equals in the land of their birth is simply amazing to me. When I was growing up in South Africa, this would have been unthinkable.

So as I stood in Westminster Abbey at the great service of

thanksgiving for Nelson Mandela, I rejoiced, but I also wept. I wept for the pain, the cost, the suffering, the wounds which were borne and carried, and are still borne and carried by so many South Africans. Many suffered and sacrificed so much in order that we might see this day, this democratic South Africa. I carry in my heart the names of many who paid a terrible price in those years of the 1970s, 1980s and early 1990s.

I think of Phakamile Mabija, who joined the Anglican Church's Nomad team of youth leaders, working as a non-racial team in churches and youth groups across South Africa. In July 1977 Phakamile was detained in Kimberley by the security police and held under the Riotous Assemblies Act. On 7 July 1977 it was reported that he had plunged to his death from the sixth floor of the Transvaal Road police station in Kimberley. Today Transvaal Road has been renamed Phakamile Mabija Road.

I think of Victor Afrikander, a parish priest in the Pietermaritzburg area and a good friend to me. On 4 May 1990 Victor was driving out of his rectory gate, taking the daughter of a friend to school. He was shot in cold blood through the head by a gunman who had been waiting for him outside the gate. Victor had been working for reconciliation in a tense and often violent conflict that had erupted in and around his parish of Imbali. I stood with other clergy later that morning and watched as the blood was washed from the front seat of his car with a hose pipe.

I think of S'khumbuzo Mbatha, community worker for PACSA (the Pietermaritzburg Agency for Christian Social Awareness), who was gunned down in Pietermaritzburg on 8 February 1992, after a meal with some US American visitors and PACSA colleagues. I was myself a trustee of PACSA in the early 1980s and helped organise and distribute fact sheets about poverty, malnutrition, forced removals and detention without trial to white churches and congregations in the Pietermaritzburg area. This was not generally popular or well received, but it was vital work if the Church was to be faithful to the authentic call of Jesus Christ.

The founder of PACSA was Peter Kerchoff, who, in 1978, left his work in a large aluminium company to set up an agency to raise awareness about issues of social justice among white South African Christians. As a member of the first PACSA committee, I shared with Peter and his wife, Joan, and a small group of local Christians in those early days of setting up PACSA. Peter was ordained a deacon in the Anglican Church in Natal. I personally know of no one who has more fully shown to me the ministry of a deacon, living as a servant of all for the sake of Jesus, than Peter Kerchoff. He was extraordinarily courageous. He knew the risks he was taking, but nonetheless he cared for and visited the families of political detainees, and he drove to the sites of forced removals to take photographs and to be alongside those who were being forcibly moved from their homes because of the Group Areas Act. Many South Africans like Peter and Joan, Phakamile, Victor and S'khumbuzo were people with strong convictions about their society and about the need for transformation in the service of Christ. They took action because of their faith and their convictions. This is servant ministry. Each one of these, and their families, paid an enormous price for their obedience to what they believed. Today South Africa is a transformed nation because of people like these.

During the Mandela thanksgiving service I found myself drawn back to an awareness, a realisation, of who I am. I was born in South Africa and went to school and university there. I was formed by South Africa in the apartheid era, by the context in which I grew up. For me, being a minister, a servant of Christ, means being irrevocably called to live in a particular way, wherever I may find myself. This is a call to live as an agent of change, bound by hope, and committed to a radical discipleship in the name of Jesus for the sake of the world. I believe that as followers of Christ we are called to make a difference, to live not for ourselves but for our neighbours and for the weak and the poor. Each of us has the potential, the possibility that is given to us, to change the world in some way or other for good and for the sake of others. The converse of this is the possibility of damaging or abusing our world, through our indifference and apathy, or even through our greed and selfishness.

As I reflect on my South African experience, and the friends and colleagues that I have worked with, it seems to me that all of this starts with our own hearts. It begins with our faith, our convictions and our response to that faith, our willingness to be those in whom God's love can rule and reign. We do not give in to the deceitfulness of much of our consumerist culture; we do not simply go along with ways of living that are comfortable and cause no offence. The way of Christ is not convenient. It does not quietly conform to the prevailing winds, the established powers and authorities and their values. This is a way of life that is full of risk, that can cost a great deal, but which ultimately changes everything.

Many of those who inspired me in my student days in South Africa were Christian leaders. Men like Trevor Huddleston, David Bosch and Desmond Tutu, and women like Sheena Duncan of the Black Sash and Adelaide Tambo seemed to live out a type of spirituality that was both deeply rooted in prayer, in God and in Christ, and also utterly committed to prophetic action and opposition to apartheid. This is what I now see as contemplative ministry. This ministry begins with the care and right ordering of our own hearts, and it leads to the transformation of our society, and of the world. Nelson Mandela understood this very well. His *Conversations with Myself* includes a letter from Nelson, written to his wife Winnie Mandela in Kroonstad Prison, dated 1 February 1975.

> ... the cell is an ideal place to learn to know yourself, to search realistically and regularly the process of your own mind and feelings. In judging our progress as individuals we tend to concentrate on external factors such as one's social position, influence and popularity, wealth and standard of education. These are, of course, important in measuring one's success in material matters and it is perfectly understandable if many people exert themselves mainly to achieve all these. But internal factors may be even more crucial in assessing one's development as a human being. Honesty, sincerity, simplicity, humility, pure generosity, absence of vanity, readiness to serve others—qualities which are within easy reach of every soul—are the foundation of one's spiritual life.[54]

Honesty, sincerity, simplicity, humility, generosity, absence of vanity, readiness to serve others—Mandela is writing here about spiritual formation and spiritual disciplines. The working out of this inner discipline in Mandela's life was highly significant in the transformation of the nation he came to lead. Instead of retribution and violence, there was forgiveness and reconciliation. At the service in Westminster Abbey, Desmond Tutu spoke about the way in which South

Africans have taken the path of reconciliation and forgiveness. Archbishop Desmond said, 'It was because he, who spent 27 years in jail, came out transformed from the angry militant to the magnanimous leader who believed we each had the capacity to be great, to be magnanimous, to be forgiving, and to be generous. We cannot give up on anyone. We all have the capacity to be saints. The veneration that we saw worldwide at his death is because he made us believe that we were made for goodness, for caring, for loving, for laughter, for peace such as the Agnus Dei proclaims.'[55]

The call to be an ordained minister in the Anglican Church in South Africa provided for me a compelling vision of a life to be lived in the service of Christ for the sake of others. When a young man once asked me about my experiences of being ordained as a priest, I said to him, 'There are three reasons why it has been good for me to be ordained. First, I get to do a lot of servant ministry, like visiting the sick, whether I like it or not. Second, I am paid by the Church to pray. Third, they don't pay you very much; you're never going to get rich as an Anglican priest, and I thank God very much for that.'

This is a life of prayer and an ever-deepening relationship with God, of servant ministry and living simply for the sake of others. We walk this path so that our hearts may be taught the ways of humility, integrity, simplicity, generosity and the readiness to serve others. This leads to the ministry of reconciliation, and from there to transformation. This is the life of Jesus, the life of the disciple, the life of contemplative ministry. For me, it is the greatest of privileges. I have known what it is to journey together with a great company of fellow Christ-followers, and we have seen God do a mighty work of transformation, the healing of our nation of South Africa, and for that we give thanks to God.

Conclusion:
Returning to the beginning

IN 2005 I was Rector of St Peter's, Yaxley, and going through a difficult time. The church needed to change and move forward, but there was much resistance. I was worn down by the conflict and difficulty. One Sunday morning, after three services, I was standing at the church door, waiting to lock up and go home. The churchwarden walked up to me and handed me an envelope. 'Here's my resignation, Ian,' he said. I was stunned. He said that he didn't agree with the changes that were happening, and this would be his last Sunday as churchwarden.

I walked home in a daze. I put down my books in my study, got into my car and drove. I found my way to Little Gidding, in the Huntingdonshire countryside, about ten miles from Yaxley. The church at Little Gidding had become an important place for me, a place I could go and somehow know that God was there. In that church the distance between the present and the eternal seemed very thin. It had become for me a place of being close to God.

On the walls of the church at Little Gidding are words from the poem 'Little Gidding' by T.S. Eliot, which is part of the *Four Quartets*.

You are not here to verify,
Instruct yourself, or inform curiosity
Or carry report. You are here to kneel
Where prayer has been valid.[56]

In 'Little Gidding' T.S. Eliot describes the contemplative journey. Contemplative prayer is not about verifying or instructing ourselves. It is the journey from the head to heart, from knowledge to that which is beyond knowledge, that which is deeper than facts and instruction and measurement.

As we are drawn to the contemplative way of life, we are drawn to the mystery that is God, the One who is beyond words, beyond formulas and boxes and categories. Our human intellect cannot contain God. We can know God in Christ Jesus, and the fire of the Holy Spirit is kindled in human hearts. Equally we cannot know God. He is indeed very great, the Creator of all things; 'such knowledge is too wonderful for me' (Psalm 139:6). He is the inscrutable, ineffable One who does not give account to us for what is and what is not. We strive, we suffer, we cry out, we kneel before him because he is God alone, and ultimately we are lost without him. In our emptiness we come to God, in the prayer that is beyond words, where all that we do is to be present—the 'now' meeting with the eternal.

In encountering this mystery that is God, we find ourselves led by the Holy Spirit to discover our true selves. We are released from that which held us when we were young adults, the ego, the claims of the false self, of power and control, and we move towards detachment. We let go, and we let God become God in our inner being. It is the flame of the Holy Spirit, the Spirit of truth and love that purifies and sets us free.

We return to the beginning, the place where we started, and we know the place for the first time. I dimly remember when I was a child, a little boy, standing on an iron bathtub, talking to the world, playing and happy, knowing that I belonged in the world and that the world was made for me. I was loved then; my place was secure, but not for long. Within me there is a longing to find that boy again, to return, to become the self I once was. Can this ever be? We shall not cease from exploration, but we are being led by love, and if we will follow we will find that which our hearts are seeking. This is the promise of Jesus to us.

Notes

1 Richard Foster, *Celebration of Discipline*, Hodder & Stoughton, 1980, p. 13.
2 *Reform* July/August 2012.
3 J.R.R. Tolkien, *The Lord of the Rings*, HarperCollins, p. 339.
4 Joan Chittister, PACSA Newsletter, December 1991.
5 Thomas Merton, *No Man is an Island*, Burns & Oates, 1955, p.103.
6 Thomas Merton, *New Seeds of Contemplation*, New Directions, 1972, pp. 34–35.
7 Richard Rohr, *Adam's Return*, Crossroad, 2004, p. 43.
8 Merton, *New Seeds of Contemplation*, p. 35.
9 Billy Connolly, *The Times Magazine*, 27 September 2008.
10 John Adair, *How to Find Your Vocation*, Canterbury Press, 2000, p. 4.
11 *The Times*, 1 February 2014.
12 Thomas Merton, *New Seeds of Contemplation*, New Directions, 1972, p. 31.
13 Bill Hybels, *Courageous Leadership*, Zondervan, 2002, p. 185.
14 Eugene Peterson, *Under the Predictable Plant*, William B. Eerdmans, 1992, p. 49.
15 Walter Brueggemann, *Spirituality of the Psalms* , Fortress Press, 2002, p. 8.
16 Richard Rohr, 'Contemplation and Compassion: The Second Gaze', *The Bible in Transmission* , Bible Society, Summer 2009.
17 Evagrius Ponticus, *Chapters on Prayer*, Sr. Pascale-Dominque Nau, Rome, 2012, p. 21.
18 Ponticus, *Chapters on Prayer*, p. 17.
19 Theophan the Recluse, quoted in Henri Nouwen, *The Way of the Heart*, Ballantine Books, 1981, p. 59.
20 Ponticus, *Chapters on Prayer*, p. 35.
21 *The Way*, Campion Hall, Oxford OX1 1QS, April 2014, p. 18.

22 Ponticus, *Chapters on Prayer*, p. 44.

23 Ponticus, *Chapters on Prayer*, p. 26.

24 *Cruden's Complete Concordance*, Zondervan, 1967, p. 290.

25 Henri Nouwen, *The Way of the Heart*, Ballantine Books, 1981, p. 60.

26 Taken from Common Worship: Services and Prayers of the Church of England © The Archbishops' Council 2000.

27 David Watson, *One in the Spirit*, Hodder & Stoughton, 1973, p. 9.

28 Bob Dylan, *Chronicles Volume One*, Simon & Schuster, 2004, p. 20.

29 Andrew Judge, email letter dated 21 June 2014.

30 *The Sunday Times*, 6 July 2014.

31 Stefan Kiechle, *The Art of Discernment*, Ave Maria Press, 2005, p. 52.

32 God's Politics blog, http://sojo.net/blogs, Jim Wallis, June 2013.

33 Thomas Keating, *Open Mind, Open Heart*, Continuum, 1986, p. 168.

34 Keating, *Open Mind, Open Heart*, p. 169.

35 David Jenkins, Bampton Lectures 1966.

36 John Dalrymple, *Letting Go in Love*, Darton, Longman & Todd, 1986, p. 58.

37 James Finley, 'From a dialogue with Dr James Finley about letting go', with Stephanie Raffelock, *The Contemplative Way Newsletter*, August 2013.

38 Jeremy Taylor, *The Rule and Exercises of Holy Living*, accessed on Google Books, p. 2.

39 Keith Egan, quoted in Philip Sheldrake (ed.), *The New SCM Dictionary of Christian Spirituality*, SCM Press, 2013, p. 211.

40 Taylor, *The Rule and Exercises of Holy Living*, p. 2.

41 Stephen A. Macchia, *Crafting a Rule of Life*, InterVarsity Press, 2012, 14.

42 Esther de Waal, *Seeking God*, Fount Paperbacks, 1984, p. 99.

43 *The Rule of Taizé*, Les Presses de Taizé, 1968, p. 6.

44 Joan Chittister, *Wisdom Distilled from the Daily: Living the Rule of St Benedict Today*, Harper One, 1990, p. 28.

45 Richard Foster, *Celebration of Disciple*, Hodder & Stoughton, 1980, p. 1.
46 Foster, *Celebration of Discipline*, p. 8.
47 Jim Wallis, *The Call to Conversion*, Lion Publishing, 1981, p. 7.
48 Henri Nouwen, *Spiritual Formation*, SPCK, 2001, p. xvi.
49 Nouwen, *Spiritual Formation*, p. v.
50 Nouwen, *Spiritual Formation*, p. 115.
51 www.givewell.org .
52 Henri Nouwen, *The Wounded Healer*, Doubleday, 1979, p. xvi.
53 Henri Nouwen, *In the Name of Jesus*, Darton, Longman & Todd, 1989, p. 22.
54 Nelson Mandela, *Conversations with Myself*, Macmillan, 2010, p. 211.
55 www.westminster-abbey.org (sermons).
56 T.S. Eliot, 'Little Gidding', *Collected Poems 1909–1962*, Faber & Faber, 1963, p. 222; in the USA copyright 1940 by Houghton Mifflin Harcourt Publishing Company; copyright © renewed 1968 by T.S. Eliot. Reprinted with permission of Houghton Mifflin Harcourt Publishing Company. All rights reserved.

Dreaming of Home

Homecoming as a model for renewal
and mission

Michael Mitton

Finding a sense of 'home', a special place of acceptance and belonging, is a fundamental human longing. In this powerful and profound book, Michael Mitton shows how it is in fact an essential part of both personal development and spiritual renewal. Drawing on his own experience of the 'homecoming' journey, he considers how we can go about finding our true home within God's eternal kingdom, how to identify the forces within us that may hinder this search, and the importance of churches offering a welcoming home to all.

Each chapter concludes with questions for personal reflection or group discussion and the book also features an imaginative retelling of the parable of the Prodigal Son, addressing some of the issues raised through a story-based approach.

ISBN 978 1 84101 877 5   £7.99
Available from your local Christian bookshop or direct from BRF:
please visit www.brfonline.org.uk

Also available for Kindle: see www.brfonline.org.uk/ebooks.

Rhythms of Grace

Finding intimacy with God in a busy life
Tony Horsfall

Rhythms of Grace emerges from a personal exploration of contemplative spirituality. Coming from an evangelical and charismatic background, Tony Horsfall felt an increasing desire to know God more deeply. At the same time, he felt an increasing dissatisfaction with his own spiritual life, as well as concern at the number of highly qualified and gifted people involved in Christian ministry who experience burn-out.

In this book he shows how contemplative spirituality, with its emphasis on realising our identity as God's beloved children and on being rather than doing, has vital lessons for us about discovering intimacy with God. It also provides essential insights about building a ministry that is both enjoyable and sustainable.

ISBN 978 1 84101 842 3   £7.99
Available from your local Christian bookshop or direct from BRF: please visit www.brfonline.org.uk.

Also available for Kindle: see www.brfonline.org.uk/ebooks.

Enjoyed
this book?

Write a review—we'd love to hear what you think.
Email: reviews@brf.org.uk

Keep up to date—receive details of our new books as they happen.
Sign up for email news and select your interest groups at:
www.brfonline.org.uk/findoutmore/

Follow us on Twitter @brfonline

By post—to receive new title information by post (UK only), complete
the form below and post to: BRF Mailing Lists, 15 The Chambers, Vineyard,
Abingdon, Oxfordshire, OX14 3FE

Your Details	
Name _____	
Address_____	
_____	
Town/City _____	Post Code _____
Email _____	

Your Interest Groups (*Please tick as appropriate)	
☐ Advent/Lent	☐ Messy Church
☐ Bible Reading & Study	☐ Pastoral
☐ Children's Books	☐ Prayer & Spirituality
☐ Discipleship	☐ Resources for Children's Church
☐ Leadership	☐ Resources for Schools

Support your local bookshop
Ask about their new title information schemes.